The Prime Minister & the Cabinet

Paul Fairclough

Advanced
Topic*Master*

Series editor
Eric Magee

10

For Clare, Adele and Felicity

Philip Allan Updates
Market Place
Deddington
Oxfordshire
OX15 0SE

Orders
Bookpoint Ltd, 130 Milton Park, Abingdon, Oxfordshire, OX14 4SB
tel: 01235 827720
fax: 01235 400454
e-mail: uk.orders@bookpoint.co.uk
Lines are open 9.00 a.m.–5.00 p.m., Monday to Saturday, with a 24-hour message answering service. You can also order through the Philip Allan Updates website: www.philipallan.co.uk

Printed in Spain

Philip Allan Updates' policy is to use papers that are natural, renewable and recyclable products and made from wood grown in sustainable forests. The logging and manufacturing processes are expected to conform to the environmental regulations of the country of origin.

P00830

Contents

Whatever happened to the cabinet?

Do we have 'presidential government'?

Introduction

About this book

This book sets out to explore the complex relationship between the prime minister and cabinet, whilst at the same time recognising the importance of other individuals and bodies, both within the core executive and beyond. In so doing, it seeks to address the elusive question of precisely where power lies within the British system of government.

Each chapter in this study takes the form of an essay that addresses a single theme in the debate, posed as a question.

Chapter 1 identifies the origins and scope of prime ministerial power, whilst identifying the various formal and informal roles that the modern premier is required to perform. In addressing the question of 'how extensive' the powers of the prime minister are, this chapter inevitably introduces some of the factors that limit the premier's freedom of action.

The second chapter develops upon these ideas by providing a more detailed analysis of the various limitations on prime ministerial power. In this way it introduces some of the themes that are central to the presidential thesis addressed in Chapter 6.

Chapter 3 considers recent developments at the heart of government, particularly recent changes in the nature and structure of the Cabinet Office and the Prime Minister's Office. In so doing, it addresses the question of whether or not Tony Blair has created something akin to the US West Wing (i.e. a 'Prime Minister's Department') within Downing Street.

The fourth chapter provides a link between our initial focus on the prime minister and the assessment of cabinet that follows in Chapter 5. It identifies four factors that have contributed to the ongoing debate surrounding prime minister–cabinet relations and sets the scene for the discussion of the various models of executive power evaluated in Chapter 6.

Chapter 5 introduces and assesses the traditional notion of cabinet government before moving on to consider the way in which certain factors have permanently and fundamentally changed the very nature of cabinet.

The final chapter uses the knowledge and understanding developed in earlier chapters to evaluate the various models of executive power advanced in recent years. Particular attention is given to the question of whether or not the UK has in effect now moved from a parliamentary system of government to something more akin to a presidential one.

Terms defined in the glossary have been highlighted in purple the first time they appear for easy reference.

Further study

At the end of each chapter you will find a number of tasks designed to test and develop your understanding of the issues raised. Each chapter also includes a list of accessible articles that will help you consider different perspectives and explore some of the themes raised in the text more fully.

Extra information on the prime minister and cabinet can be found by studying the relevant chapters in the kinds of general politics textbook readily available in school, university or public libraries. There are, in addition, a number of well-regarded topic-specific texts that might be of interest to those looking to dig a little deeper. The following may be of particular use:

- Bagehot, W. (1867) *The English Constitution*, Fontana [1963].
- Burch, M. and Halliday, I. (1996) *The British Cabinet System*, Prentice Hall.
- Foley, M. (1993) *The Rise of the British Presidency*, Manchester University Press.
- Hennessy, P. (1986) *Cabinet*, Blackwell.
- Hennessy, P. (1996) *The Hidden Wiring*, Indigo.
- King, A. (1985) *The British Prime Minister*, Macmillan.
- Rhodes, R. A. W. and Dunleavy, P. (1995) *Prime Minister, Cabinet and Core Executive*, Macmillan.
- Rose, R. (2001) *The Prime Minister in a Shrinking World*, Polity.

There are a number of websites that might also prove useful. The *Guardian* site (www.guardian.co.uk) allows users to search for archived articles using key words. The full versions of many of the articles used in this book can be obtained in this way, along with more up-to-date articles and editorials. The main UK government portal (www.direct.gov.uk) also provides a range of helpful links to other government sites, notably the 10 Downing Street site (www.number10.gov.uk) and the Cabinet Office site (www.cabinetoffice.gov.uk). Students looking to extend their studies further might consider some of the research papers available from parliament (www.parliament.uk/parliamentary_publications_and_archives/research_papers.cfm).

Paul Fairclough

How extensive are the powers of the prime minister?

Though Walter Bagehot famously argued that the prime minister was merely *primus inter pares* (first among equals), the years since the publication of his seminal 1867 work *The English Constitution* have increasingly seen commentators of all shades take a rather different view. The modern prime minister is seen as all powerful. Indeed, it is argued, the president of the USA, shackled by the separation of powers and a system of entrenched checks and balances, might reasonably envy the freedom of action afforded to the UK premier.

The irony is, of course, that regardless of the powers granted to each individual and the apparent weight of the checks that operate upon them, so much remains dependent upon the incumbent's ability and circumstance. Thus, while former prime minister Herbert Asquith famously asserted that 'the office of the prime minister is what its holder chooses and is able to make of it', former US president,' Woodrow Wilson could just as easily conclude that 'the president is at liberty, both in law and in conscience, to be as big a man as he can. His capacity,' Wilson concluded, 'will set the limits.'

We will return in later chapters to the debate over precisely how much of a prime minister's power comes by virtue of the office and how much remains dependent upon the incumbent's abilities. Our aim at this early stage is simply to identify precisely what powers the prime minister possesses in his or her armoury, and the basis of such powers.

Sources of prime ministerial power

The prime minister's powers are drawn from three overlapping sources:
1 powers formally assigned to the monarch under the royal prerogative, but now exercised by the prime minister on the monarch's behalf
2 powers that have developed over time through convention

3 powers normally afforded to the prime minister as leader of the majority party in the House of Commons

The royal prerogative

The term 'royal prerogative' is usually applied to those powers once held by the monarch in common law (see Box 1.1). Through the passing of parliamentary statute and the emergence of new conventions, most of these powers have now been transferred either in law or in practice to the prime minister or to parliament. The ability of the prime minister to assimilate prerogative powers since the turn of the seventeenth century has been a key feature of the development of the office.

Box 1.1

The royal prerogative before the 1689 Bill of Rights

- The power to make laws by proclamation (i.e. without parliament).
- The power to make war, conclude treaties and command the armed forces.
- The power to call and dissolve parliament.
- The power to create peers of the realm and to select judges, Church of England bishops and other high officials.

The importance of convention

Though the assimilation of the prerogative powers has been the most significant process by which the UK prime minister's position has been defined and extended, one should not underestimate the extent to which the office has developed through convention. It is, after all, by convention rather than under statute that many of the prerogative powers have passed into the hands of the premier. It is also through convention that citizens, party, parliament, cabinet and key officials have come to submit themselves to prime ministerial authority, to a greater or lesser extent.

The prime minister as party leader

Another crucial convention is that the leader of the majority party in the Commons is offered the job of prime minister by the monarch following a general election — and that the same individual will lose this position in the event that he/she loses the confidence of that chamber. This convention, intertwined with the development of coherent and disciplined parties since the 1850s, has provided a key source of prime ministerial power and authority. The importance of this link between the post of prime minister and that of party leader is emphasised by the fact that those who are forced to give up the leadership of their party (e.g. Margaret Thatcher in 1990) must also give up the keys to No. 10. The prime minister's power and authority rests, therefore, upon the confidence of the Commons which, with a majority government, is in turn dependent upon the confidence and support of those sitting on the prime minister's own benches.

The roles of the prime minister

The absence of a codified constitution formally detailing the prime minister's various roles and powers has inevitably led commentators to draw up their own lists. This should come as no surprise; even in the USA, where presidents are formally assigned the role of chief executive in Article II of the constitution, other roles — for example, those of 'chief legislator' and 'head of state' — have developed over time through convention.

Though writers such as Neil McNaughton (Box 1.2) and Dennis Kavanagh (Box 1.3) may differ in respect of the labels they choose to apply to the various roles performed by the UK premier, they agree on many if not all of the broad areas in which the prime minister is required to act. For both authors, the role of party leader is key. Similarly, McNaughton's identification of 'government leader' and 'economic manager' is in large part analogous to Kavanagh's roles of 'head of the executive' and 'head of government policy'.

Though the models proposed by McNaughton, Kavanagh and others each have their own strengths, there is clearly some merit in our advancing a clear and authoritative list of our own as a means of providing some markers for the discussion of prime ministerial power that follows. For our purposes, the roles of the modern prime minister are fivefold:

1 chief executive
2 chief legislator
3 chief diplomat
4 public relations chief
5 party chief

> **Box 1.2**
>
> **McNaughton on the roles of the prime minister**
>
> - policy making and implementation
> - leading the nation
> - leading the government
> - leading the party
> - economic manager
>
> Source: McNaughton, N. (1999) *The Prime Minister and Cabinet Government*, Hodder.

> **Box 1.3**
>
> **Kavanagh on the roles of the prime minister**
>
> - head of the executive
> - head of government policy
> - party leader
> - head appointing officer
> - party leader in parliament
> - senior UK representative overseas
>
> Source: Jones, B., Kavanagh, D., Moran, M. and Norton, P. (2004) *Politics UK* (5th edn), Pearson.

The extent of prime ministerial power

Having isolated the sources of prime ministerial power and the roles that the modern premier is expected to perform, we can now move on to consider the powers the incumbent has to hand when discharging his or her duties. Attempts to catalogue and classify the powers of the prime minister have been as numerous and as varied as the efforts made to identify discrete roles. Some have chosen to identify a range of powers as a means of supporting or refuting a broader model of executive power (see Box 1.4). Others, such as Tony Benn have sought to provide a degree of codification, by providing a clear and authoritative list (see Box 1.5).

Box 1.4
R. A. W. Rhodes on prime ministerial power

'Advocates of the prime ministerial power thesis argue that the Prime Minister is more powerful than the cabinet because he or she is the leader of the party, has the power to appoint and dismiss ministers, chairs the cabinet and controls its agenda, has more opportunity to amass considerable personal popularity with the electorate through skilled use of the media, appears on the international stage as a world leader and because freedom from departmental responsibilities enables him or her to intervene over the full range of government policy.'

Source: Rhodes, R. A. W. and Dunleavy, P. (1995) 'Prime ministerial power to core executive' in *Prime Minister, Cabinet and Core Executive*, Macmillan.

Box 1.5
Tony Benn's ten elements of prime ministerial power

- power to appoint, reshuffle or dismiss ministers
- power to create peers
- power over honours generally
- power to appoint chairmen of nationalised industries
- further powers of appointment
- power over ministerial conduct
- powers relating to the conduct of government business
- powers over information
- powers in international relations
- powers to terminate a parliament or government

Source: Benn, T. (1981) *Arguments for Democracy*, Jonathan Cape.

Despite the differences of approach between Rhodes, Benn and the others who have attempted to provide an inclusive list of prime ministerial power, it is possible to identify five broad areas on which all might agree. We might refer to these areas as the five facets of prime ministerial power:

1 powers of patronage
2 powers over cabinet, government and civil service
3 powers over parliament
4 powers over agenda setting and policy making
5 powers on the world stage

Powers of patronage

One aspect of the prime minister's role as *de facto* chief executive is that the office holder possesses considerable powers of patronage, such as the power to:

- appoint and dismiss ministers at cabinet level and below
- appoint senior civil servants (including senior diplomats, members of quangos, special advisors and heads of nationalised industries)
- appoint bishops in the Church of England
- create peers
- appoint senior judges
- nominate individuals for the honours list

These powers are based firmly upon the royal prerogative. However, where it was once the case that the monarch would appoint ministers and senior officials, the administration is now 'Her Majesty's Government' in name only, with the prime minister distributing the baubles largely as he or she sees fit.

Though one should not underestimate the importance of the historical role played by the prime minister in the appointment of bishops, peers and judges, it is the appointment of government ministers and civil servants that demands the closer scrutiny.

How extensive are the prime minister's powers over ministerial appointments, at cabinet level and below?

The simple answer to this question is, of course, 'very'. In theory at least, the prime minister is at liberty to appoint whoever he or she likes to high office, provided that they are drawn from parliament. Indeed, the prime minister can, as we will see, bring people into parliament purely as a means of offering them positions within government. It is generally accepted, however, that a prime minister's freedom of patronage as regards government posts is limited by the need to provide balance and maintain unity.

At the time of the 2001 general election, *The Economist* identified a number of criteria that might come into play when bringing an administration together (see Box 1.6).

Box 1.6

Framing a cabinet

Gender A need to balance the cabinet in terms of gender, particularly in light of the large number of women MPs in the Commons since 1997.

Ethnicity As with gender, a desire to reflect the broader society by bringing in some members from ethnic minorities.

Guilt The sense that prime ministers may try to reward those who have lost out badly in previous reshuffles.

Personality A need for at least one or two individuals with genuine charisma within cabinet, alongside more worthy but dry administrators.

Political balance A desire to reflect the political spectrum of the broader party within cabinet.

Source: adapted from 'New Labour, (some) new faces', *The Economist*, 24 May 2001.

We might easily broaden the issue of 'guilt' to include 'reward' and 'loyalty'. Few attain cabinet rank without having first demonstrated a willingness to follow the party **whips** almost without question.

One might also add another criterion, that of ability, to the list provided. Though UK cabinet members are normally generalists, unlike their US counterparts, prime ministers generally look to appoint those who have demonstrated the intellect and organisational ability necessary to manage a government department. Most cabinet members will, therefore, have served an apprenticeship as junior minister before elevation to high office. Most, though not all, will also come to office with a reputation as experienced and capable parliamentarians. As Ian Budge noted, therefore, 'once the political has-beens, the never-will-bes, and those with difficult political and personal histories have been ruled out, the prime minister may be left with rather little choice' ('The prime minister, the cabinet and the core executive', in Budge, I., Crewe, I., McKay, D. and Newton, K. (2004) *The New British Politics*, Pearson).

Can prime ministers 'fire' any more easily than they can 'hire'?

While, on the face of it, prime ministers can dispense with the services of government colleagues as they see fit, dismissing ministers can, in fact, be just as hard as appointing them. Though Harold Macmillan was willing and able to remove around one-third of his cabinet in July 1962 — in the so-called

Night of the Long Knives — and Margaret Thatcher was never afraid to force out those who were not, as she put it, 'one of us', recent occupants of Number 10 have appeared far less willing to wield the axe. John Major took 8 months to bow to the inevitable and replace Chancellor Norman Lamont in the wake of 'Black Wednesday' in 1992 — despite Lamont's offer to resign at the time of the crisis — and Blair was similarly reluctant to move against his allies (such as David Blunkett) and his critics (such as Clare Short).

This change in approach is easily explained. Though a prime minister is free to use power to fire and reshuffle creatively, there is always the danger of creating a backlash. After all, those in post are likely to have allies elsewhere in the government, or on the back benches. Increasingly, prime ministers look to avoid dismissing ministers who are demonstrably failing for fear of the problems that they might cause once stripped of their departmental responsibilities and the obligation to uphold the doctrine of collective responsibility. In addition, it is worth noting that neither Macmillan nor Thatcher was able to silence dissenting voices within his or her party by demoting them or forcing them from their posts. In both instances, the premiers' aggressive use of their powers of patronage was a sign not of their strength, but of their failing authority.

Power over cabinet, government and civil service

Though the prime minister's power over the cabinet is greatly enhanced by the ability to promote or demote political allies and potential rivals, the premier's powers over cabinet, government and civil service do not stop there.

Powers within cabinet

The modern prime minister has a range of powers over and within cabinet, above and beyond the powers of patronage (see Figure 1.1). The prime minister determines the number, the timing and the duration of cabinet meetings. For

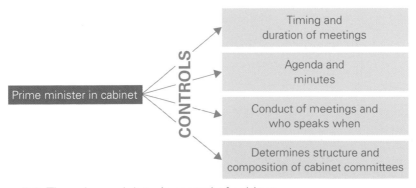

Figure 1.1 The prime minister's control of cabinet

example, whereas cabinet meetings may once have lasted for several hours, former cabinet minister Mo Mowlam noted Tony Blair's preference for far shorter sessions. More significantly, perhaps, the prime minister's control over the number and duration of meetings has a direct bearing on the kind of work that can be reasonably attempted within meetings.

Thus, whereas in 1867 Walter Bagehot saw the cabinet as a decision-making body — the 'efficient secret' of the English constitution — Mowlam argued that the cabinet had been reduced to the status of a mere talking-shop or briefing room under Blair, with the real decisions being taken elsewhere. Though senior cabinet colleagues could certainly push for longer and/or more frequent meetings, the prime minister would be under no obligation to concede to their demands.

The prime minister's control of the agenda, the name, number and order of speakers, and the process of summing up at the end of meetings and producing minutes, also gives the incumbent the ability to steer cabinet discussion in the direction that he or she wants it to go, and away from areas that may prove more problematic. Margaret Thatcher was said to be particularly adept at manipulating the 'running order' at cabinet meetings in such a way as to make more

likely her favoured outcome. The failure to allow proper cabinet discussion of issues close to member's hearts can certainly lead to public conflict; witness Michael Heseltine's departure from the post of defence secretary over the Westland affair in 1986 or the eventual departure of Robin Cook (March 2003) and later Clare Short (May 2003) over the UK action in Iraq. Such instances of cabinet rebellion are, however, clearly the exception rather than the rule. The underlying and implied threat of dismissal or demotion is normally sufficient to ensure that ministers submit themselves to the prime minister's authority.

Margaret Thatcher was said to be particularly adept at manipulating the 'running order' of cabinet meetings

The final area in which the prime minister controls cabinet, namely the freedom to determine the number and nature of cabinet committees, is clearly crucial to any understanding of the extent of the prime minister's power. With full cabinet meetings now shorter and less frequent, it is inevitable, as we have already noted, that these full meetings will alter in nature. Hence the tendency for the cabinet to become an arena for ministers to brief colleagues on developments in their area, rather than a genuine decision-making body. It follows, therefore, that if cabinet is no longer making decisions, these decisions must be being made somewhere else, whether it be in cabinet committees or in **bilateral meetings** between the prime minister and a single cabinet colleague. With the prime minister obviously in a position to determine whom he meets in such bilateral meetings (the **'sofa-government'** of Blair's first term), his control of the composition and chairmanship of cabinet committees helps tie up the remaining loose ends.

Powers over government

Many of the points that we have made in respect of prime ministerial control of cabinet can also be applied in the context of the premier's control of the government as a whole. Though the 80 or so ministers of various rank outside of the cabinet are not formally tied to the doctrine of cabinet collective responsibility to the same degree as their more senior colleagues, they are certainly expected to remain loyal. Those wishing to oppose government policy would generally be expected to give up their office in order to do so. This means that lower government ministers, like their cabinet colleagues, owe their position to the prime minister and know that their continuance in office depends upon their loyalty.

Though prime ministers may be reluctant to return those with genuine ability to the back benches, governments with large Commons majorities have at least some room for manoeuvre when dishing out the minor jobs. With a parliamentary party of around 400, the party of government will normally have around three **backbenchers** to every minister. Though some backbenchers will already have served their time in office (Budge's 'has-beens') and others will be unwilling or unsuitable for promotion through the ranks (the 'never-will-bes'), the prime minister clearly has options, even if the pool from which he or she must choose is more limited than it might at first appear.

Through the powers of appointment to lower government positions, the prime minister also has the central role in departmental team building. The premier can shuffle people in or out of departments in such a way as to elevate allies and marginalise rivals. The prime minister can also place loyalists in departments in order to keep an eye on potential rivals within the cabinet.

Powers over the civil service

The prime minister has extensive powers over the upper reaches of the civil service. These powers can be broadly divided into those relating to patronage and those concerned with management and coordination.

As chief executive, the prime minister exercises considerable powers of patronage over senior civil service appointments, most notably at the level of permanent secretary. Whereas the UK civil service was once said to be founded on the three principles of impartiality, anonymity and permanence, with candidates supposedly promoted on merit, recent years have witnessed a process of overt politicisation in the upper reaches of the bureaucracy; not only in respect of regular civil service appointments but also through the proliferation of special advisors following Labour's election to office in 1997. With key civil servants and special advisors increasingly involved in what would once have been considered 'party political matters', the prime minister's role in appointing such officials is crucial to his or her control of the core executive.

This process has been most obvious in the reorganisation and expansion of the work of the Cabinet Office in recent years. The creation of new Cabinet Office bodies such as the prime minister's Delivery Unit and the Better Regulation Executive has seen a blurring of the line between those concerned with civil service administration and the prime minister's personal advisors and staff. In all of this, the role of individuals such as the cabinet secretary has been crucial. The prime minister's relationship with the cabinet secretary is at the heart of prime ministerial control of the modern bureaucracy. The parallel development of the Prime Minister's Office since 2001 has led some to herald the emergence of a US-style 'West Wing' in Downing Street. Such developments, dealt with more fully in Chapter 3, have given the prime minister significant powers in managing and coordinating the work of the administration.

Power over parliament

Analyses of the power of the prime minister over parliament commonly start with a discussion of the relationship between executive and legislature in the UK, as compared to that in the USA. In the UK, it is argued, the fusion of the two branches means that the prime minister is 'in parliament' whereas in the USA the membership of the two branches is constitutionally required to be separate. Thus the president is not a member of Congress.

In reality, the situation is somewhat different. Recent prime ministers have effected an informal separation between themselves and the legislature, not least through their infrequent attendance and poor voting records. For writers such as Michael Foley, this is an aspect of spatial leadership — the way in which the prime minister separates himself from other institutions and from cabinet colleagues, thereby becoming more presidential.

Far more significant than the prime minister's physical presence in parliament is the range of powers the premier has over membership and management of the legislature. These powers draw in part on the royal prerogative, but also on the role of party leader identified earlier.

The prime minister's powers of patronage under the royal prerogative offer a significant degree of control over parliament. Both in the Commons and in the Lords, the prime minister appoints key figures. The leader of the House of Commons, for example, plays a crucial role in managing the work of the chamber, coordinating the timetabling of bills and setting the times when parliament sits. The use of patronage also allows the prime minister to alter the composition of the upper chamber. The removal of all but 92 of the hereditary peers following the passage of the 1999 Lords Reform Act cleared the way for Labour to appoint a large number of life peers in their place. The result has been that a chamber with an in-built majority of 600 broadly conservative peers has been transformed into one which, by 2 May 2006, had more peers taking the Labour whip (207) than any other (the Conservatives had 204). Though the Lords can still provide an effective check on the power of the prime minister, this shift in the balance of power, and the government's increased willingness to resort to the Parliament Act (see Box 2.9 on p. 30), means that the prime minister is normally able to get his or her bills through.

Prime ministers also have considerable control of the membership of the Commons through their role as party leader. Their position as leader enables them to fast-track political allies through the process of candidate approval and short-listing and on into the Commons through elections in safe seats. In recent years this route has seen a significant number of former special advisors find their way into the Commons, with several quickly making the move on into ministerial positions (see Table 1.1).

| Table 1.1 | Former Labour special advisors in the Commons following the 2005 general election |

Name	Constituency	Safest Labour seat by majority
David Miliband	South Shields	38th
Ed Miliband	Doncaster North	41st
Pat McFadden	Wolverhampton SE	58th
Ed Balls	Normanton	121st
Kitty Ussher	Burnley	223rd
Ian Austin	Dudley North	241st

Source: Fairclough, P., Kelly, R. and Magee, E. (2006) *UK Government and Politics Annual Survey 2006*, Philip Allan Updates.

The prime minister can also use his or her powers as party leader to parachute individuals into constituencies directly (as happened with former Conservative MP Shaun Woodward in St Helens in 2001), or to force out those who go too far (e.g. Labour's National Constitutional Committee expelling George

Galloway from the party in 2003, despite support for the MP in his Glasgow constituency Labour Party).

The prime minister's control of the parliamentary party through the whips' office means that he or she can normally be sure of a safe passage for bills. Though ostensibly these are still 'government bills', we have already seen the way in which the prime minister's control of the various centres of policy making might allow a capable incumbent to dominate the process. It is the cumulative weight of these powers that see the premier take on the role of chief legislator.

Power over agenda setting and policy making

As we have seen, the prime minister's control of the executive and his or her ability to control parliament through powers of patronage and powers as party leader give the incumbent a key role in agenda setting and policy making. It is, after all, the prime minister who is largely responsible for the Queen's Speech, and the measures outlined at the state opening of parliament are normally expected to be approved in their entirety.

There is, however, another means by which the prime minister's role in agenda setting has been enhanced: the rise of the mass media. Though the monarch remains the formal head of state, it is clear that the last 20 years have seen the rise of the prime minister as a key public figure — the government's and perhaps the nation's senior spokesperson; the 'communicator in chief'. In the same way that US presidents from Franklin D. Roosevelt onwards have used their 'fireside chats' and set-piece broadcasts to engage directly with citizens, the prime minister has also become a focus for the nation. It was, after all, Tony Blair, not the queen, who mirrored the public reaction to Diana Princess of Wales's death — referring to her as the 'people's princess' in his official statement — and the modern prime minister is always well to the fore when national unity is needed (e.g. in the closing stages of the 2012 Olympic bid campaign or in the wake of the 7 July bombings in 2005).

Whether it is the rise of the mass media that has facilitated the emergence of more media savvy politicians, or a new generation of charismatic communicators who have granted the media access as a means of extending their own influence, is a moot point. We are clearly no longer in an age where Clement Attlee could respond 'No' to a BBC reporter who asked whether he could explain Labour's plans for the 1955 general election campaign. The nation now demands more of its chief executive, and the prime minister is therefore granted unrivalled access to media that are anxious to know what he or she thinks. A capable incumbent can use this access to his or her advantage, whether to refocus the political agenda or to support or undermine other politicians. Those who are less comfortable in the public eye are unlikely even to become a party leader, yet alone prime minister. Opinion polls regularly rank leaders in terms of whom the voters would most like to be prime minister, and the general election is increasingly run as a popularity contest between the leaders of the two biggest parties, despite the fact that only those voters who live in the leader's constituency will ever be able to vote for him or her.

Power on the world stage

When John Major negotiated the terms of the UK's acceptance of the Maastricht Treaty in 1992, it was widely assumed that the agreed treaty would require some kind of parliamentary ratification before it became binding. This would certainly be the case in other western liberal democracies. In many European states, the treaty was subject to popular consent by referendum. In the USA the president requires the support of two-thirds of the Senate in order to ratify any treaty he negotiates on the nation's behalf.

In reality, however, the prime minister's powers on the world stage are based largely upon the royal prerogative as opposed to statute (see Box 1.7). Though Major chose to submit the Maastricht Treaty to a Commons vote, there was no need to do so, as his legal counsel had confirmed. It was legally binding as soon as he had signed it.

Box 1.7

Prerogative powers on the world stage

The conduct of foreign affairs remains reliant on the exercise of prerogative powers. Parliament and the courts have perhaps tended to accept that this is an area where the Crown needs flexibility in order to act effectively and handle novel situations. The main prerogative powers in this area include:

- the making of treaties
- the declaration of war
- the deployment of the armed forces on operations overseas
- the recognition of foreign states
- the accreditation and reception of diplomats

Source: Commons Public Administration Select Committee, Press Notice No. 19, Session 2002–03.

The prime minister's power to wage war is similarly founded on prerogative powers long-since transferred from the monarch. No monarch has led his or her army into battle since George II at Dettingen (1743). The modern prime minister is truly commander-in-chief, free to commit UK forces as he or she sees

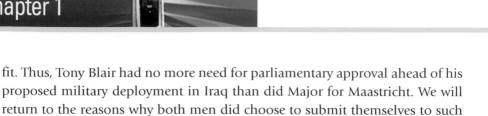

fit. Thus, Tony Blair had no more need for parliamentary approval ahead of his proposed military deployment in Iraq than did Major for Maastricht. We will return to the reasons why both men did choose to submit themselves to such a vote (even referring to these votes as 'questions of confidence' and hinting that they might resign if defeated) in Chapter 2.

Alongside the assimilation of prerogative powers, the rise of a modern mass media has been central to the emergence of the prime minister as a serious player on the world stage. It is clear that the modern prime minister speaks on behalf of the nation in the same way that the US president does in his capacity as *de facto* head of state. Even though the prime minister has not concurrently held the post of foreign secretary since the days of Ramsey MacDonald (to 1929) or before him Salisbury (to 1900), it is common for the prime minister to take the lead over the individual formally assigned control of the Foreign Office. At the time of the Falklands War it was Thatcher, rather than her foreign secretaries, Carrington and Pym, who took key decisions such as whether or not to sink the Argentinean battleship, the *General Belgrano*, and it was largely Thatcher who took the public credit for the liberation of the islands. Similarly, it was Blair, rather than his then foreign secretary, Jack Straw, who took the lead over Iraq. It was clearly a 'Blair–Bush Axis' as opposed to a 'Straw–Powell' or 'Straw–Rice' one (despite the latter pair's much reported evening out in Blackburn). Moreover, it is the prime minister whom the public expect to speak at such moments. Premiers who choose to remain silent or are otherwise indisposed are often subject to a public backlash.

Conclusion

The above discussion would appear to suggest that the powers available to prime ministers are indeed extensive and are becoming increasingly more so. As we have already seen, however, no proper assessment of the extent of prime ministerial power can be complete without an understanding of the limitations acting upon the premier. In Chapter 2 we will explore these limitations more fully.

Task 1.1

Study the sources of prime ministerial power identified at the start of this chapter.

(a) Explain what is meant by the term 'prerogative powers'.

(b) Why is the role of party leader so crucial to any understanding of prime ministerial power?

Task 1.1 (continued)

Guidance

(a) It is important to adopt a systematic approach when answering these types of question. First, you must provide a clear and authoritative definition of the term in question. Second, you should spend a little time explaining the scope of prerogative powers — using a range of appropriate examples to add depth to your analysis. Finally, you should make an effort to pick up on the debate surrounding the prime minister's use of prerogative powers (e.g. questions of accountability, democracy and legitimacy). It might be helpful to divide your discussion along domestic policy/foreign policy lines.

(b) On a simple level, the prime minister's very position as chief executive is based upon his or her leadership of the majority party in the House of Commons. You need to move beyond this, however, to consider how the premier can use the position of party leader to control government and the legislature.

Task 1.2

Use the information in this chapter to produce a detailed spider diagram on the powers of the prime minister, based on the outline structure provided below.

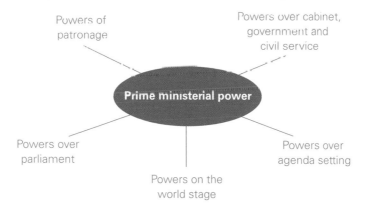

Guidance

It is probably better to complete your diagram on A3 rather than A4 paper so that you can get the necessary detail into each section without losing clarity. You should outline the range of powers available to the prime minister in each area and provide appropriate examples to illustrate each point. You might want to try to add connecting lines between different areas of power where you think that it is appropriate.

Task 1.3

Obtain an up-to-date list of cabinet members. Research some basic biographical information relating to each individual and study carefully Box 1.6 on p. 10.

(a) Using the information obtained, for each member copy and complete the table below.

Choosing a cabinet

Cabinet member	
Gender	
Ethnicity	
Reward for loyalty or guilt	
Personality	
Political balance	
Ability (experience or intellect)	

(b) Are you aware of any individuals on the governing party's back benches who might be more deserving of a place in cabinet? If so, why are they not there?

Guidance

(a) You should be able to get an up-to-date list of cabinet members from the No. 10 website (**www.number-10.gov.uk**) or the Cabinet Office website (**www.cabinet-office.gov.uk**). Potted biographies of current cabinet members can be found on the Politics section of the BBC website (**http://news.bbc.co.uk/1/hi/uk_politics**).

(b) It will always be possible to find those on the back benches who appear better qualified for high office than those in post. Once you have identified one or more individuals who fall into this category, you need to think about why they are not in government. It might help to think again about some of the areas we have looked at in Chapter 1, such as the need to balance the cabinet in terms of ideology, gender or geography. You should also consider factors such as willingness to serve and whether or not the individual in question has served in cabinet previously.

Further reading

- Garnett, M. (2005) 'Still first among equals?', *Politics Review*, vol. 14, no. 4.
- Kavanagh, D. (2001) 'Tony Blair as prime minister', *Politics Review*, vol. 11, no. 1.

How effective are the limitations on prime ministerial power?

We made reference to some of the limitations operating upon the modern premier when setting out the extent of prime ministerial power in Chapter 1. The purpose in this chapter is to provide a more thorough assessment of such constraints by grouping them into five categories (see Box 2.1).

> Box 2.1
> **A prime minister constrained?**
>
> **1** Limited by **cabinet**?
> **2** Limited by **parliament**?
> **3** Limited by **party**?
> **4** Limited by **public opinion**?
> **5** Limited by their **abilities** and by **circumstance**?

Prime ministerial power and the cabinet

As already discussed, the prime minister's powers over cabinet are considerable, both in respect of its composition, and in its structure, organisation and procedure. It would clearly be naïve, however, to suggest that a group with so much experience and ambition should be totally at the whim of one of their number.

Can the cabinet remove the prime minister?

The way in which the roles of cabinet and prime minister have evolved, specifically the absence of a codified constitution, has meant that there is no formal mechanism by which the cabinet can remove the premier. In this respect, the

UK is unusual. Even in the USA, where the cabinet has hardly taken a central role in recent decades, the 25th Amendment allows the vice-president to declare the president 'unable to discharge his duties' and replace the incumbent, where he can garner the support of a majority of the 'principal officers of the executive departments' (i.e. 'Secretaries of State').

Similarly, though the prime minister, like the US chief executive, can be removed through impeachment proceedings — a fate some thought Tony Blair deserved, following the decision to deploy troops in Iraq (see Box 2.2) — the cabinet would have no real role in such a process.

Box 2.2
Impeaching the prime minister

'General Sir Michael Rose, commander of UN forces in Bosnia in 1994, writes in today's *Guardian*: "The impeachment of Mr Blair is now something I believe must happen if we are to rekindle interest in the democratic process in this country once again." Britain was led into war on false pretences, he says. "It was a war that was to unleash untold suffering on the Iraqi people and cause grave damage to the West's prospects in the wider war against global terror." '

Source: Norton-Taylor, R. (2006) 'Impeach Blair on Iraq, says general', the *Guardian*, 10 January.

In the modern era, therefore, the closest we have come to a cabinet 'removing' the prime minister was when Margaret Thatcher resigned as leader of the Conservative Party (and, therefore, as prime minister) in 1990. In that instance, the prime minister consulted cabinet colleagues one by one ahead of a planned second ballot in the leadership contest. Their almost unanimous advice that she should step down was, by her own admission, the deciding factor.

In what ways can the cabinet limit the prime minister's powers of appointment?

As we have seen, the prime minister's choice of cabinet members is limited by the need for balance, and by the talent and suitability of those willing to serve. Certain senior party figures are, it is commonly argued, guaranteed key positions at the cabinet table. In reality, senior key cabinet members may also influence the rise and fall of others. Under Blair, for example, it was notable that those fast-tracked into office were not all allies of the prime minister. Senior Brownites, such as former special advisor Ed Balls, were installed in safe Commons seats in the 2005 general election and groomed for ministerial positions. Following the 2005 general election, senior cabinet members such as

Charles Clarke and John Prescott were also said to have moved to block David Blunkett's return to the cabinet at the head of a new 'super ministry' governing communities, fearing that their own ministries would be diminished. Blunkett was eventually forced to accept a more modest position as work and pensions secretary.

The start of Blair's third term saw a prime minister apparently being forced into lengthy negotiations regarding the make-up of his team, and even then not entirely getting his way (see Box 2.3).

Box 2.3

Reshuffle by negotiation?

'Tony Blair has recently pointed to his continuing power of patronage to back his claim that he will maintain his authority in his third term, despite his plan to stand aside near its end.

But the Prime Minister began in the worst possible way in the aftermath of Thursday's election with a reshuffle that displayed weakness and ineptitude. One of his closest supporters and a veteran of many botched Blair reshuffles said yesterday it was never a good idea to have a reshuffle by negotiation — and that is what it looked like.'

Source: Wintour, P. (2005) 'Weak PM forced to negotiate changes to team', the *Guardian*, 9 May.

In what ways can cabinet challenge the prime minister's control of decision making?

Prime ministers' control over policy making within the executive is, as we have seen, highly impressive, through their control of cabinet meetings, their domination of cabinet committees (see Chapter 5) and the Cabinet Office (see Chapter 3), and their ability to take discussions to the sofas of No. 10 in bilateral and trilateral meetings.

There are, however, a number of avenues open to senior cabinet colleagues who want to seize the initiative. At a simple level, cabinet members can submit items for inclusion on the agenda for cabinet meetings. Though cabinet meetings have, as we have seen, changed in nature over the last decade, it remains a convention that certain core areas of policy and contentious or topical issues will appear on cabinet agendas as a matter of course. Under Blair, for example, three items were commonly included on cabinet agendas:

1 a report on parliamentary business
2 a report on economic and home affairs
3 a report on foreign affairs

European business had been taken as a separate agenda item under Major — a nod perhaps towards those Eurosceptics in cabinet and within the broader parliamentary party — but Blair took EU issues under the three broader agenda headings from 1999.

How easy, then, is it for cabinet members to force discussion on the issues that concern them during these 'briefings'? Though, in most cases, only senior cabinet members would be allowed to interrupt the weekly briefings in order to engage those present in more general debate, Garnett and Lynch have rightly argued that ministers can still have a significant input in certain circumstances (see Box 2.4). In such instances, ministers may be invited to give their views, though they may still have to put a powerful case, brief the press or threaten resignation in order to 'bounce' the prime minister into a course of action that he or she does not wish to take. Indeed, in recent years any number of major decisions have been taken with little or no cabinet discussion (see Box 2.5).

Box 2.4
Grounds for genuine cabinet discussion?

- Issues are especially important or sensitive.
- Major issues or unexpected developments require a rapid decision.
- Government departments and ministerial committees have been unable to reach agreement.

Garnett, M. and Lynch, P. (2003) *UK Government and Politics*, Philip Allan Updates.

Box 2.5
Decisions taken outside of cabinet

Margaret Thatcher The final decision to push ahead with the introduction of the community charge (the **'poll tax'**) was taken in a cabinet committee rather than in full cabinet.

John Major The prime minister's 1993 **'Back to Basics' campaign** was launched with little or no cabinet discussion.

Tony Blair Only four senior ministers were involved in taking the decision to hand control over interest rates to the Bank of England. Blair was also said to have left the cabinet discussing the Millennium Dome in order to attend a press conference announcing the government's support for the project.

The perceived absence of a process of genuinely collective decision making in cabinet invariably results in ministers' unwillingness to abide by the doctrine of collective cabinet responsibility. The result of this process has been ministers' willingness to brief the press 'off the record'. In his autobiography, for example,

John Major spoke of 'the bastards' undermining his authority from the inside, and Tony Blair faced a similar fate after 2005 over issues such as education reform and healthcare.

The threat of resignation — either explicit or implied — is often enough to force the prime minister to back down on questions of policy. In the case of the UK's joining the exchange rate mechanism, for example, Margaret Thatcher was essentially forced to submit by her Home Secretary Geoffrey Howe's and her Chancellor Nigel Lawson's threat of joint resignation in June 1989. Such a strident approach does not always work, however. In 1986 Michael Heseltine eventually chose to leave the cabinet — mid-meeting — over his failure to secure full cabinet discussion of the Westland affair. Though it is argued that cabinet ministers might join together to threaten mass resignations in the face of a particularly intransigent premier, the reality is that the personal ambitions of those in office, and the internal cabinet rivalries that arise from these ambitions, are normally strong enough to allow the prime minister the freedom to divide and rule.

Michael Heseltine's cabinet resignation, 1986

Prime ministerial power and parliament

Though the prime minister is dependent upon parliament for the passage of all of his or her government's legislation, and also for the very continuance of the government itself, the premier is rarely placed under serious pressure in either respect. Control of the majority party in the Commons, together with the various conventions and statutes that limit the powers of the Lords, normally ensures safe passage of government bills through their various readings. Committee action is similarly limited both in scope and scale, and is subject to the same party whipping that dominates proceedings on the floor of the Commons (see Box 2.6).

> Box 2.6
>
> **The Whip's Office and the prime minister**
>
> - Each of the main parties has a Whip's Office in the Commons.
> - The governing party's Whip's Office is staffed by a chief whip — appointed by the prime minister in his or her capacity as party leader — and around 12 assistants.
> - The whips circulate a document called the Whip, which indicates the importance the party attaches to each measure set to come before the House by the number of times it is underlined.
> - The Whip's Office is responsible for maintaining party discipline in the House. It can recommend those who are loyal for promotion and impose sanctions on rebels.
> - The ultimate sanction a rebel may face is the withdrawal of the whip. This means that the MP is expelled from the parliamentary party.

With prime ministerial control of parliament so dependent upon the premier's control of his or her party in the lower chamber, many have argued that the effectiveness of parliamentary checks on the chief executive is directly linked to the size of the prime minister's Commons majority (see Table 2.1). Thus, it is said, parliament was a more effective limitation on the powers of John Major after the 1992 general election than it had been during Margaret Thatcher's second term. In a similar vein, some argued that Tony Blair would be more limited by parliament following losses in the 2005 general election than he was after the emphatic victories of 1997 and 2001.

Table 2.1 Majorities of incoming governments, 1979–2005

Election	Prime minister	Majority
1979	Thatcher	43
1983	Thatcher	144
1987	Thatcher	101
1992	Major	21
1997	Blair	179
2001	Blair	165
2005	Blair	65

This analysis, though appealing, is rather too simplistic. First, it is wrong to assume that the prime minister is more likely to experience catastrophic rebellions when his or her parliamentary majority is small than when it is larger. Backbenchers may, in fact, be more loyal at times of small Commons majorities, for fear of precipitating a government defeat that might in turn result in a general election that would see them losing their own seats. In contrast, backbenchers in a large parliamentary party, who may see little chance of immediate promotion, may become more complacent and, therefore, be more likely to rebel. At the same time, prime ministers with small majorities often become far more versed in avoiding defeat, whereas those with large ones (e.g. Thatcher, Blair) may feel that they don't need to make the effort to carry their backbenchers with them (see Box 2.7).

Box 2.7

Labour rebellions, 1997–2005

In his work on Commons rebellions (**www.revolts.co.uk**) Philip Cowley has gone some way towards showing that Labour backbenchers under Blair (1997–2001) were not the 'poodles' they were often portrayed as in the media. Indeed, even with the Commons majority of 165 secured in the 2001 general election, the government only secured passage of the bill that introduced top-up fees with a majority of 5. This compares to the 40-vote majority that John Major secured in the 'confidence vote' over the Social Chapter provisions of the Maastricht Treaty in July 1993.

Second, the focus on the size of Commons majority ignores the fact that the House of Lords (see below) can present a far more serious obstacle to the government's programme than the various limitations imposed by the Commons.

Third, it is unlikely that the various opposition parties will unite against the party of government in order to defeat legislation. It would, for example, require a particularly strange set of circumstances or a government in total disarray to see parties from both sides of the sectarian divide in Northern Ireland pass through the same lobby as nationalists in Scotland and Wales and the MPs from whichever two of the three larger UK parties are in opposition. Indeed, it is not uncommon to see one of the larger opposition parties backing the government on policy in a vote where they might otherwise have forced an embarrassing defeat (see Box 2.8).

Box 2.8

Saved by the official opposition?

In 1994 Labour MPs abstained on the second of the two 'confidence' votes called by Major, resulting in a government majority of 214. Tony Blair has also benefited from opposition support. In the 2003 vote on Iraq, for example, Conservative MPs largely backed the prime minister's position. Similarly, the 2006 Education and Inspections Bill was only passed as a result of the backing of Conservative and Democratic Unionist MPs after a major backbench Labour rebellion. Philip Cowley argues that the bill might easily have been lost (267:258) without such support.

With such observations in mind, we can move on to consider some of the supposed parliamentary limitations on the prime minister.

Prime Minister's Questions

The former twice-weekly Prime Minister's Questions (PMQs) sessions in the Commons were always said to be more theatre than politics. Blair's decision to move from two 15-minute sessions on Tuesdays and Thursdays to a single half-hour slot on Wednesdays was heralded as a move to allow more careful scrutiny of the premier and reduce the tendency towards 'yah-boo politics'. Ultimately, neither objective has really been achieved, though the live television and radio coverage of the weekly event has probably not helped in this respect. PMQs remains a contest where the leaders of the two major parties endeavour to secure points, as opposed to landing a knockout blow, in a bout scheduled to last 100 or more 300-minute rounds, spread over a period of 4–5 years. Though the failure of opposition party leaders such as Iain Duncan Smith and Menzies Campbell to perform effectively at PMQs damaged their standing within their

respective parties, those who succeed in embarrassing the prime minister at PMQs are no more likely to see their Wednesday victories translated into votes at the ballot box (witness William Hague). At best, PMQs is a forum in which the prime minister may feel slight discomfort, though we should remember that many of his or her answers, like the questions themselves, are well scripted in advance.

Tony Blair responding to questions in the House of Commons

The vote of confidence

Given the fact that there has been no formal vote of confidence in a government since James Callaghan's administration was defeated and thereby obliged to resign from office in 1979, it is remarkable just how much emphasis is placed upon this mechanism. Though the size of the Commons majority is not, as we have seen, always a reliable guide to the likelihood of serious backbench rebellion in the chamber, it is rare indeed for governments possessing any kind of working Commons majority to face any real threat from a vote of confidence. Put simply, the risks for backbenchers are too high. A rebellion by backbenchers in the majority party that forced the government from office would see all MPs facing a general election. In such circumstances, a party that was so disunited would be expected to lose a considerable number of seats. It would, therefore, be the very backbenchers who had voted their party out of government who would stand to lose most. After all, cabinet members tend on the whole to have safer seats than their backbench colleagues.

Far from the vote of confidence being a tool with which the Commons can limit the prime minister, it is — more often than not — a device that is turned against potential rebels by the prime minister. As we noted in Chapter 1, both Major and Blair hinted that they regarded key votes — over Maastricht and Iraq respectively — as votes of confidence and might resign were they to lose. For backbench Conservative Eurosceptics the threat was clear: either vote for Maastricht or see the prime minister resign and/or seek a general election in which the party might face catastrophic losses. Major's logic was certainly compelling; as one cartoon caption put it at the time, 'Fly me to Maastricht or I'll kill us all'.

The prime minister and the Liaison Committee

Though standing and special committees in the USA play a considerable role in limiting the power of the president, UK parliamentary committees do not have the same resources or powers available to them. They cannot, for example, subpoena the prime minister or other ministers as a means of ensuring their attendance. Thus the Commons Public Administration Select Committee failed in its attempt to persuade Blair to give evidence before it on the Ministerial Code in 2001, though he later agreed to be questioned by the Commons Liaison Committee twice each year. These biannual meetings, conducted in the Boothroyd Committee Room in Portcullis House, have provided a genuine opportunity for MPs to question the prime minister outside of the theatre that is PMQs. In the February 2006 session, for example, the prime minister was quizzed on issues as varied as the UK's presidencies of G8 and EU, the government's reform agenda as regards healthcare and schools, relations with Iran, and the likely fallout from elections in Palestine.

The prime minister and the House of Lords

The Lords lack many of the powers of scrutiny afforded to the US upper chamber. After all, the prime minister does not require Lords' confirmation for senior appointments. Neither is he or she required to seek the chamber's approval for the ratification of treaties. In addition, the removal of the in-built majority of Tory peers through the House of Lords Act (1999) and the existence of the Parliament Act and the Salisbury Doctrine (see Box 2.9) would seem to

Chapter 2

suggest that the House of Lords should present a far less effective limitation upon the powers of prime minister and government than does the Senate on the US executive.

Box 2.9
Some limitations on the Lords

The Parliament Acts, 1911 and 1949

The 1911 Parliament Act replaced the Lords' right to veto legislation with the power to delay bills for 2 years. At the same time, the Lords were effectively prevented from vetoing, amending or delaying money bills. The Parliament Act of 1949 reduced the power of delay to one parliamentary session.

The Salisbury Doctrine

Dating from 1945 the Salisbury Doctrine put in place the principle that the Lords — as an unelected chamber — should not oppose government bills at second reading where the government had established a clear electoral mandate to act by including a measure in its manifesto.

The reality of the situation is somewhat different, however. The UK second chamber has proved a major obstacle to government legislation over the last 25 years. The various Conservative administrations were defeated in Lords' votes on 241 occasions between 1979 and 1997 with 155 of these defeats taking place during Margaret Thatcher's time in office. In an age of comfortable Commons majorities (see Table 2.1), many came to regard the Lords as the 'real opposition' within parliament, and all of this at a time when the Conservatives were said to have an inbuilt majority of around 350 peers over Labour. Labour's decision to remove the hereditary peers following its election victory in 1997 was, in part at least, a reaction to its fears of the style of Lords' obstructionism that had frustrated earlier Labour administrations. That said, Labour has still faced significant Lords opposition since the 1999 Lords Reform Act over issues as diverse as fox hunting, university top-up fees and ID cards. The government — and by implication the prime minister — was defeated on amendments on a total of 101 occasions between 2003 and 2005 (see Table 2.2).

Table 2.2   Government defeats in the Lords

	Amendments		Government defeats
	Tabled	Passed	
2003–04	9,602	3,344	64
2004–05	3,306	913	37
Totals	12,908	4,257	101

Faced with such opposition, the Blair government demonstrated a willingness to compromise at times (e.g. over anti-terrorist legislation since the attacks of 11 September 2001), but they were also increasingly willing to invoke the Parliament Act (see Box 2.9) where compromise proved undesirable or impossible. Though the Parliament Act was not used at all in the 50 years following its amendment in 1949, and only once prior to Labour coming to power in 1997 (over the 1991 War Crimes Act), it was used on three occasions between 1999 and 2005:

1 European Parliamentary Elections Act (1999)
2 Sexual Offences (Amendment) Act (2000)
3 Hunting Act (2004)

It is the last of these uses, in outlawing hunting with hounds, that is of most relevance to our discussion here as it led to a legal challenge that, while failing in its central aim, brought into question the way in which the Parliament Act might be used in the future (see Box 2.10). This ruling, coupled to suggestions that opposition parties in the Lords might be less willing to abide by the Salisbury Doctrine and the news that the Lords would be investigating the prime minister's use of prerogative powers, appeared to offer the prospect that the Lords might become a rather more effective check upon the ambitions of the premier.

Box 2.10

Limits on the Parliament Act

'Senior ministers are bracing themselves for a fresh showdown if the Law Lords endorse a [February] ruling [from the Court of Appeal] challenging the government's right to overrule the upper house. Though the court upheld the legality of the use of the 1949 Parliament Act to force through a ban on hunting, the court concluded that "the greater the scale of the constitutional change proposed, the more likely that it would fall outside the powers contained in the 1911 Act". This could leave a question mark over the government's ability to use the Parliament Act to remove the remaining 92 hereditary peers.'

Source: adapted from the *Guardian*, 3 August 2005.

Tony Blair's reaction to such pressures included the suggestion that continued obstructionism on the part of the Lords might result in the Salisbury Doctrine being given statutory force, with peers barred from rejecting measures originating in the governing party's manifesto. The prime minister also instructed Lord Falconer, then the secretary of state for constitutional affairs, and Lord Goldsmith, the attorney general, to reject the suggestion that MPs might be

given a vote in advance of any future military action. 'The government's position,' Falconer confirmed, 'is that…formal constraints, in statute or convention, do not work when faced with the reality of planning a deployment.'

How much are prime ministers limited by their party?

The existence of majority government in the UK means that the prime minister's control of his or her party is often taken as being analogous with control of parliament. Though we have already established that the size of a government's majority is not everything, it is certainly the case that the prime minister's control of his or her party's MPs (however large the Commons majority) is crucial.

Thus, prime ministers who face serious opposition in parliament normally arrive at such a position because they have lost their own back benches. Similarly, the loss of the back benches often comes as a result of the prime minister losing the confidence of cabinet colleagues and/or the broader public. Although parliamentary parties tend to avoid attacking the prime minister openly for fear of a public backlash against a visibly divided party, recent times have seen backbenchers more willing to articulate their concerns. The Conservatives' 1922 Committee of backbenchers raised concerns over the leadership of Margaret Thatcher at the end of the 1980s — in the face of the then lowest opinion poll ratings ever achieved by a premier and with cabinet divisions clear for all to see — and the Parliamentary Labour Party (PLP) was similarly keen to put its views to Tony Blair, over both Iraq and the domestic reform agenda, either side of the 2005 general election. Blair was said to have given assurances that he would take on board lessons learnt on the doorstep during the campaign and 'listen more'.

How easy is it for the party to remove its leader while in office?

Between 1989 and 1995 the party in office, the Conservatives, challenged their leader — and, therefore, the prime minister — on three occasions. In 1989 and 1990 Margaret Thatcher was challenged first by the 'stalking horse' Anthony Meyer and then by former defence secretary Michael Heseltine. This second contest, in which the prime minister narrowly failed to secure the margin of victory required to avoid a second ballot, eventually led to her resignation and the election of John Major as party leader and, therefore, prime minister. In

1995, John Major himself survived a leadership challenge by former Welsh secretary John Redwood. Such examples give the impression that the majority party in the Commons can be a significant check on the premier, through its power to replace him or her as party leader and thereby remove their right to hold the position of prime minister.

In reality, however, the likelihood of a prime minister being removed by a party leadership challenge has receded somewhat in recent years as a result of changes in Labour and Conservative Party rules. Between 1981 and 1988 Labour MPs wishing to challenge their leader required the support of just 5% of the parliamentary party. Since 1989, however, challenges to an incumbent Labour prime minister have needed the support of 20% of the PLP and a two-thirds majority vote at the annual conference. Though rumours spread of a possible leadership challenge to Blair in 2006 — a result, it was said, of the prime minister's refusal to name the date when he would step down — such a challenge to an incumbent Labour prime minister would now be extraordinarily difficult to execute. Similarly, the Conservatives have learnt a good deal from the internal divisions of the 1980s and 1990s. They would probably be far less willing to challenge a leader while the party is in office. In 1990, Michael Heseltine only required the support of two MPs (one to nominate and another to second his nomination) in order to challenge Margaret Thatcher. As part of William Hague's Fresh Future initiative in 1998, however, the party made significant changes to the system by which the leader is challenged. Though leadership hopefuls would only need the support of 15% of the party's MPs to instigate the process with a vote of confidence, the incumbent would only need to secure the support of the majority of his or her colleagues in order to remain in office, avoiding the formal leadership election that might otherwise have followed.

How easy is it for the party to influence the prime minister's choice of cabinet members?

Prime ministers certainly have to take note of opinion on the back benches when making cabinet appointments. It would be unwise, for example, to leave those with significant support festering on the back benches where they might easily become the focus for other disaffected members. It has always been the case, therefore, that prime ministers look to bring such figures on board, perhaps acknowledging the ancient Chinese general Sun Tzu's belief that it is advisable to 'keep your friends close, and your enemies closer'. Thus, John Major chose to include not only leadership rival Michael Heseltine (as deputy prime minister) but also Eurosceptics Michael Portillo and John Redwood. Under Blair, Clare Short, another MP who had a strong backbench following, was able

to retain her position as secretary of state for international development despite the fact that she had publicly questioned agreed cabinet policy over Iraq. Conversely, Margaret Thatcher's problems certainly intensified once she had forced figures such as Heseltine, Nigel Lawson and Geoffrey Howe out of government, where they could be required to uphold the doctrine of collective responsibility, and on to the back benches. It was ultimately Heseltine's 1990 leadership challenge that precipitated the end of the Thatcher premiership.

In the Labour Party, the rank and file have an even greater input into the composition of the cabinet when the party is returning to government following a period in opposition. The Labour Party rules state that in such circumstances the first cabinet should be comprised largely of those who had previously been elected to the shadow cabinet. Thus when Labour returned to office in 1997, 17 members of the cabinet had been elected to the party's shadow cabinet in July 1996.

This rule aside, a prime minister is always free to ignore party favourites if he or she so chooses, as long as the premier is prepared to accept the serious consequences that may follow.

How easy is it for the party to influence the prime minister and government over policy?

Backbench members of the governing party are clearly in a position to appeal on matters of policy to those of their colleagues who hold government positions. In 1992, for example, John Major was placed under extreme backbench pressure over Maastricht. His efforts to silence those who opposed his approach eventually resulted in eight Conservative backbenchers (later known as the 'Whipless Wonders') having the whip removed. After the 2005 general election Tony Blair also came under pressure from those on the left of the Parliamentary Labour Party who argued that it was time for the party to return to something more akin to traditional 'old Labour' positions in the wake of sweeping losses.

There was a time when those beyond the parliamentary parties would also present a significant limitation on the prime minister's control of policy through the process by which the parties themselves formulated policy. This was particularly true in the case of the Labour Party where, before Blair, a policy securing a two-thirds vote at the annual conference automatically went into the party programme and — more often than not — the manifesto. In 1997, however, the party moved to a 2-year policy cycle whereby the National Policy Forum appointed policy commissions to make proposals which were then formalised within the National Executive Committee (NEC) before being passed on to the party conference for final approval. Though this change was aimed at producing more considered policy and avoiding the kind of public rows that had become common at the annual party conferences, some saw it as a thinly veiled attempt by the leadership to gain greater control over the policy-making process and avoid nasty surprises.

In the Conservative Party, the leader still has the major role in policy making, though the leader is expected to take some notice of the views of backbenchers (as represented by the 1922 Committee), party elders, members of the front bench and the broader membership. The Fresh Future initiative launched by William Hague following the 1997 general election defeat was supposed to make policy making more inclusive. Two new bodies — the National Conservative Convention and the Conservative Political Forum — were formed, but both remained merely advisory. Hague did make use of ballots of the members to endorse his policies, but these votes were all on issues and at times chosen by him, where he could feel more confident of success. Those who followed Hague as Conservative leader between 2001 and 2006 did little to suggest that they intended to introduce a greater degree of internal party democracy in the field of policy making. There is no reason to believe, therefore, that future Conservative prime ministers will be required to listen to their party on questions of policy any more than their predecessors, or their Labour counterparts.

Prime ministerial power and public opinion

Public opinion can have both a direct and an indirect impact on the prime minister's ability to act freely. It is clear that low public approval ratings, either generally or over a specific policy initiative, have the capacity to steer the prime minister towards or away from a particular course of action. For example, Tony Blair's decision to offer a UK referendum on the proposed EU constitution in 2005 — having initially maintained that such a public poll would not be necessary — was widely seen as bowing to public pressure.

It is also possible, however, for public opinion to influence the prime minister indirectly as those around him demand a change of tack — or even a new face at the top — in the light of worrying poll findings. The 1989 and 1990 Conservative Party leadership challenges to Margaret Thatcher were clearly driven, in part at least, by a sense of self-preservation on the back benches as the likelihood of an electoral wipe-out grew. In consequence, though the modern mass media are the vehicle through which the prime minister becomes

communicator-in-chief, this is very much a two-way street; a conduit rather than simply a prime ministerial tool. When things are going badly, the media can just as easily become the means by which popular dissatisfaction is channelled and targeted on the premier.

In the main, therefore, the modern prime minister looks to moderate his or her initiatives in line with data obtained from private party polling and/or focus groups. The tendency to try and reflect the public mood is normally far more compelling than the desire to shape it. Where prime ministers choose to confront popular opinion and strike out alone, as in the case of Thatcher over the 'poll tax' or Blair over Iraq, they take a massive risk. By facing down opposition and wearing such policies as badges of honour, they stand to lose massively when things go awry. In contrast, prime ministers who do what their polling tells them the people want are less likely to suffer badly when things go wrong.

To what extent are prime ministers limited by their abilities and circumstance?

Abilities

Though prime ministers will always have opportunities to exercise significant power, the incumbent's abilities are clearly key to fulfilling the potential of the office. Though those lacking any of the necessary abilities are unlikely to find themselves occupying No. 10, ability is clearly a matter of degree. Thus, while Richard Rose saw Tony Blair as the third of a new style of television-age prime ministers, following on from Thatcher and Major (see Box 2.11), few — certainly not Rose — would see Major in exactly the same light as the other two.

Box 2.11

Richard Rose and the emergence of the 'new style' prime minister

Rose divided modern prime ministers into three groups:

1 The 'old school' generation of Churchill, Attlee, Eden, Macmillan and Douglas Home.
2 A 'transition generation' of Wilson, Heath and Callaghan, who had been shaped by the Depression and war.

> Box 2.11 (continued)
>
> **3** 'New style' prime ministers — Thatcher, Major and Blair — who lived in a 'television age that can create celebrities overnight...[where] the box that counts is the television rather than the despatch box'.
>
> Source: Rose, R. (2001) *The Prime Minister in a Shrinking World*, Polity.

Where prime ministers are limited by their own abilities, they are also limited by what is 'doable'. The uncodified and conventional basis of prime ministerial power means that the premier is obliged to operate in a manner that is reasonable. Thus, though the prime minister is not required to secure formal ratification for treaties (as is the case for the US president), John Major chose to do so over the Maastricht Treaty as it would have been unreasonable not to. The same could be said of Blair over Iraq.

In an age increasingly obsessed with accountability and subsidiarity, successive prime ministers have also been forced to accept, and even at times propose, limitations upon their own powers as follows:

- through the devolution of power away from the centre (e.g. 'downwards' with the creation of the Scottish Parliament and 'upwards' through further EU integration)
- through transferring some of the incumbent's powers of patronage into the hands of independent commissions and other bodies (e.g. the appointments to the new UK Supreme Court as established under the 2005 Constitutional Reform Act)

Circumstance

By 'circumstance' we mean the range of contextual factors that might facilitate or inhibit the exercise of prime ministerial power. As we have seen, the size of the Commons majority and — more significantly — backbench loyalty can be crucial to the prime minister, as can the calibre and loyalty of potential rivals. As Macmillan famously noted, however, it is 'Events, dear boy. Events' that do most to shape a premiership.

Many of the kinds of event identified in Box 2.12 are largely or wholly beyond the control of the prime minister, yet they shape the political landscape and limit his or her room for

> Box 2.12
>
> **'Events, dear boy. Events'**
>
> Some contingency factors, 2000–05
>
> - climate change
> - third world debt
> - fuel protests
> - foot-and-mouth disease
> - global terrorism
> - EU expansion
> - globalisation and world trade
> - sleaze and scandal

manoeuvre. The economist John Galbraith once remarked that 'Politics is not the art of the possible [as Bismarck had earlier argued]. It consists of choosing between the disastrous and the unpalatable.' We might easily apply this maxim to our study of prime ministerial power. The domestic context, natural disasters and the actions of those outside the UK — both individually and as nations — will inevitably make it impossible for prime ministers to exercise their powers to the full. In addition, forces far greater than any nation — processes of climate change and globalisation, for example — will demand shifts in policy, as did the terrorist attacks of 9/11 in the USA and 7 July 2005 in the UK.

Terrorist attack on the World Trade Center, 2001

Conclusion

Though it would be foolish to argue that the modern prime minister is powerless in the face of the various limitations outlined in this chapter, it is clear that the dynamics of the relationship between prime minister, cabinet, parliament and the broader public is a good deal more complex than it might at first appear.

The waters have been muddied further by the way in which the bureaucratic elements of the core executive have evolved and become more focused on serving the needs of the chief executive, as opposed to the needs of the government as a whole. This will be the theme of the third chapter.

Task 2.1

(a) Explain the significance of the Parliament Acts and the Salisbury Doctrine.
(b) Why do many peers no longer believe that they should be bound by the Salisbury Doctrine?

Task 2.1 (continued)

Guidance

(a) Once again, it will be necessary to provide clear and authoritative definitions before getting too bogged down in detailed analysis. You should make reference to the Parliament Acts of 1911 and 1949, and give examples of the way in which the Act has been used in recent years. You should recognise that the Salisbury Doctrine does not have the statutory status of the Parliament Act (it is a convention) but that it has, nonetheless, provided a framework by which the Lords has operated since 1945. Again, examples would be helpful.

(b) The Salisbury Doctrine is a convention; it is not rooted in statute law. It would not, therefore, be enforceable in the event that the Lords chose not to abide by it. The doctrine was based on an acknowledgement that a part-hereditary chamber lacked the legitimacy to challenge policies for which the party in government had secured a mandate at the previous general election. The removal of most of the hereditaries from the chamber as a result of the House of Lords Act (1999) undermines this argument. Reform of the chamber has also meant that the Conservatives no longer have the in-built Lords' majority afforded by the hereditaries. Increasing tension between the elected Commons and the Lords in 2005, prompted partly by the government's increased willingness to use the Parliament Act, led some peers to suggest that the convention should be suspended. This in turn prompted some ministers to suggest that the Salisbury Doctrine might be enshrined in statute.

Task 2.2

Study the information provided in this chapter on the five limitations on prime ministerial power. Using this information, copy the table below and then extend it to include the other four checks on prime ministerial power (parliament; party; public opinion; ability and circumstance).

The limitations on prime ministerial power

By whom?	What limitations?	How likely?	Examples
Cabinet	Raise matters at cabinet meetings	Difficult for an individual cabinet member to place items on the cabinet agenda	Heseltine over the Westland affair, 1986
	Threaten resignation	A 'nuclear option' only, as it seriously risks one's own career whatever the short-term outcome	Geoffrey Howe and Nigel Lawson over the exchange rate mechanism, 1989

Task 2.2 (continued)

Guidance

Do not feel that you have to cram every single word in this chapter into your diagram. What you need to do is choose one or two limitations within each area and then develop them in the 'How likely?' and 'Examples' columns. The aim of this task is that you should end up with a summary that can act as an essay plan for a question addressing the effectiveness of limitations on prime ministerial power.

Further reading

- Cowley, P. (2000) 'The marginalisation of parliament', *Talking Politics*, vol. 12, no. 2.
- Flinders, M. (2003) 'Controlling the executive', *Politics Review*, vol. 13, no. 1.

Chapter 3

Has Blair created a 'West Wing' in Downing Street?

Set over two floors, in an extension to the White House demanded by Theodore Roosevelt, the West Wing is the nerve centre of the US presidency. It contains key rooms such as the Oval Office and the Cabinet Room as well as housing the offices of many of the president's key advisors (see Box 3.1).

Box 3.1

The West Wing of the White House

The West Wing of the White House houses the US president's Oval Office, the offices of his executive staff, the Cabinet Room, the Roosevelt Room, the Situation Room and the Press Briefing Room.

Around 40–50 of the president's senior staff have offices in the West Wing. Most of the president's staff are now housed in the Eisenhower Executive Office Building, adjacent to the West Wing.

Though the constitution vested sole executive power in the hands of the president, developments since the Brownlow Committee (1937) reported that 'the president needs help' have seen a massive expansion of the presidential staff. Indeed, so many now work in support of the president that their offices can no longer be contained within the West Wing itself. Thus, while the West Wing remains a physical structure, it has also become a phrase that is used to refer to the president's staff in the broader sense. It is primarily in this context that we are posing the question of whether or not Tony Blair has created a 'West Wing' in Downing Street.

The absence of anything akin to the US West Wing in the UK before 1997 led many to suggest that the premier was at a disadvantage to his cabinet colleagues because he did not have access to the resources afforded by a ministerial department. The result of this was that examination questions commonly focused on whether or not a Prime Minister's Department should

be created. Since 1997, however, such debates have been made moot by four interconnected developments listed below:

1 a proliferation in the number of bodies, and individuals, working at the heart of government
2 the increased tendency for such individuals to be directly answerable to the prime minister
3 the increase in the number and influence of special advisors
4 the physical concentration of such offices and staff in and around Downing Street

It is these developments, and the consequences that follow on from them, that form the basis of this chapter.

Expansion and reorganisation of the Cabinet Office and the Prime Minister's Office

Has the expansion and reorganisation of bodies such as the Cabinet Office and the Prime Minister's Office contributed to the emergence of a UK 'West Wing'?

The Cabinet Office

The Cabinet Office (CO) was founded in 1916 with the creation of a series of secretariats. It was designed to help the coalition government of the time coordinate the work of government departments in response to the challenges brought by the First World War. Though the CO brought such benefits that it became a more formalised and permanent body after the Great War, it was still seen as a largely 'bureaucratic' — as opposed to a 'political' — institution until well into the 1980s.

In 1982, for example, Harvey and Bather — the then staple authors for students of 'British Constitution' — argued that the CO had seven broad roles:
1 to circulate cabinet papers, consisting of concise statements by the departments, memoranda, documents and recommendations as to the action on matters coming up for discussion
2 to prepare agendas
3 to summon persons to attend meetings
4 to record the essential points of discussion and the conclusions reached
5 to circulate these decisions to the departments affected

6 to report periodically on the implementation of decisions

7 to promote measures to remove friction between the departments

As we will see, however, the CO of the early twenty-first century is a rather different beast from the one operating for much of the twentieth. A series of structural changes brought to the office since Labour was returned to government in 1997, and the increasing overlap between the CO and the Prime Minister's Office (PMO), have led some to argue that we now have a *de facto* Prime Minister's Department.

What did the Cabinet Office look like in 2006?

Though one might think that this would be a relatively easy question to answer, the opacity of the UK core executive means that it is always difficult to pinpoint the precise organisational structure of bodies such as the CO and the PMO at any given point in time. That said, the last official organogram of the CO — published in 2003 and adapted as part of our 'Prime Minister's Department' organogram in Figure 3.1 — goes some way towards showing what an important body the CO had become.

According to the official government website there were over 20 different units within the CO in June 2005:

1 Better Regulation Executive (BRE)

2 Cabinet Office European Union Coordination Group

3 Central Sponsor for Information Assurance (CSIA)

4 Ceremonial Secretariat

5 Civil Contingencies Secretariat (CCS)

6 Corporate Development Group (CDG)

7 Defence and Overseas Secretariat

8 Development Directorate, Corporate Development Group

9 Economic and Domestic Affairs Secretariat

10 e-Government Unit (eGU)

11 Emergency Planning College (EPC)

12 European Secretariat

13 Government Chief Whip (Lords)

14 Government Communication Network (GCN)

15 Histories, Openness and Records Unit (HORU)

16 Independent Offices

17 Office of the Leader of the House of Commons

18 Office of Public Sector Information (OPSI)

19 Parliamentary Counsel Office (PCO)

20 Prime Minister's Delivery Unit (PMDU)

21 Strategy Unit

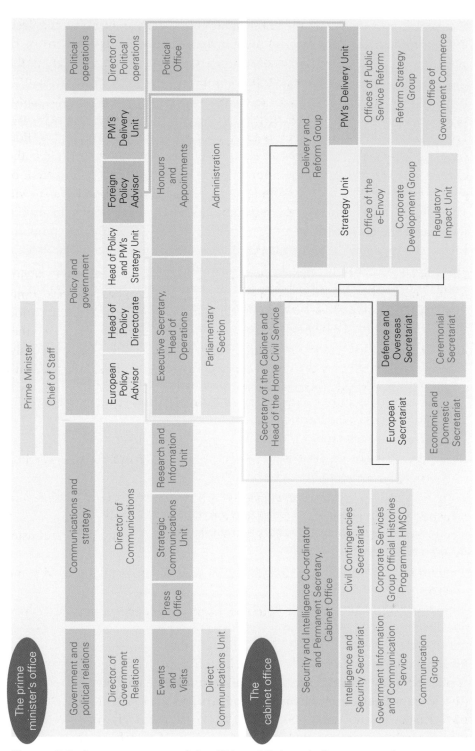

Figure 3.1 An organogram of the 'Prime Minister's Department'

The prime minister's office

Government and political relations

Director of Government Relations

Events and Visits

Press Office

Strategic Communications Unit

Direct Communications Unit

Research and Information Unit

Director of Communications

Communications and strategy

Prime Minister

Chief of Staff

Policy and government

European Policy Advisor

Head of Policy Directorate

Head of Policy and PM's Strategy Unit

Foreign Policy Advisor

PM's Delivery Unit

Executive Secretary, Head of Operations

Parliamentary Section

Honours and Appointments

Administration

Political operations

Director of Political operations

Political Office

The cabinet office

Security and Intelligence Co-ordinator and Permanent Secretary, Cabinet Office

Intelligence and Security Secretariat

Government Information and Communication Service

Communication Group

Civil Contingencies Secretariat

Corporate Services Group Official Histories – Programme HMSO

Secretary of the Cabinet and Head of the Home Civil Service

European Secretariat

Economic and Domestic Secretariat

Defence and Overseas Secretariat

Ceremonial Secretariat

Delivery and Reform Group

Strategy Unit

Office of the e-Envoy

Corporate Development Group

Regulatory Impact Unit

PM's Delivery Unit

Offices of Public Service Reform

Reform Strategy Group

Office of Government Commerce

This proliferation in the number of separate policy units and taskforces reflects the increased role that the CO now plays in coordinating the work of government. In part, the creation of such units has been made necessary by the difficulties resulting from the fact that so much of the work of government is now done in cabinet committees, as opposed to full cabinet meetings. Labour came to office in 1997 promising 'joined-up government', and the reorganisation of the CO was seen by many as a means by which a more coordinated effort could be managed. The creation of so many bodies has, however, also had the effect of further increasing the prime minister's control over the direction of government, not least because so many of those working in the CO, as we will see, are now directly answerable to the premier.

The Prime Minister's Office (PMO)

The PMO, often referred to simply as 'Downing Street' or 'No. 10', has its origins in the nineteenth century and consists of the bodies that support the prime minister in his or her day-to-day work. As is the case with the CO, the period since 1997 — and specifically since 2001 — has seen the PMO become a rather more important and more complicated structure than was the case previously. That said, the PMO is not a physical entity as in the sense of the US president's Oval Office. It instead consists of a series of units, some of which, as we will see later in this chapter, are now also part of the formal structure of the CO.

Structure of the PMO to 1997

When Labour was returned to power in 1997, the PMO that it inherited comprised four major units:

1 the **Private Office**, which managed the prime minister's engagements and helped to link the premier to the bureaucracy in Whitehall
2 the **Political Office**, which managed relations between the prime minister and his or her party
3 the **Press Office**, which managed the prime minister's relations with the media
4 the **Policy Unit**, which helped provide the prime minister with policy advice

Early changes under New Labour, 1997–2001

In Blair's first term, the PMO was altered significantly. First, the prime minister appointed a chief of staff who could manage and coordinate the efforts of those civil servants working across the various bodies in the PMO. Though Blair was not the first to create such a post — Margaret Thatcher had given David Wolfson a similar epithet between 1979 and 1985 — his chief of staff was far more than simply a titular figurehead for the PMO. Whereas Wolfson's had been more of

an informal wise counsel to the prime minister, the post of chief of staff created in 1997 was a more formal and public one, possessing considerable executive powers.

Second, Blair created three new bodies: a fifth major PMO unit, the Strategic Communications Unit; the Social Exclusion Unit (SEU); and the Performance and Innovation Unit (PIU), which was eventually merged with the prime minister's Forward Strategy Unit (see below) in June 2002. At the time of their creation, all three bodies were to report to the prime minister, despite the fact that the final two were based in the CO.

Third, there was a significant increase in the number of prime ministerial special advisors working in the PMO — a development to which we will return towards the end of this chapter.

Major restructuring after 2001

Further significant changes came in the wake of New Labour's second consecutive general election victory in 2001 (see Box 3.2).

Box 3.2
Reorganising the Prime Minister's Office in 2001

- The Private Office was merged with the Policy Unit to form the Policy Directorate.
- The prime minister's Press Secretary, Alastair Campbell, was given a new title: **Director of Communications**. Two civil service deputies took over the management of press briefings.
- Three new bodies, the Delivery Unit, the Office of Public Services Reform and the Forward Strategy Unit, were created.

Though the creation of bodies such as the Policy Directorate and posts such as Director of Communications represented evolution in the PMO rather than revolution, the creation of three entirely new bodies — the Delivery Unit, the Office of Public Services Reform and the Forward Strategy Unit — all based in the Cabinet Office, but answerable to the prime minister, was more significant:

- first, because they marked a further increase in prime ministerial power
- second, because they represented another step in the apparent merger of the CO and the PMO into something that might more closely resemble a Prime Minister's Department

The Prime Minister's Office in 2006

The last official organogram of the PMO was deposited in the Commons Library in April 2004, in response to a Parliamentary Question. This organogram (incorporated in Figure 3.1) showed the extent to which the office had been transformed since Labour was returned to power in 1997. Despite further questions in parliament (see Box 3.3), Tony Blair proved reluctant to provide an updated diagrammatic representation of his office following New Labour's third successive general election victory in 2005.

Box 3.3

In search of the Prime Minister's Office

Written Answers, Tuesday, 18 April 2006

Norman Baker (Lewes, Liberal Democrat)

To ask the Prime Minister

(1) What internal reorganisation of staff has taken place in Downing Street since May 2005; and if he will publish the staffing structures and lines of accountability in operation;

(2) If he will place an organogram of his Office in the Library.

Tony Blair (Prime Minister)

Details of the key officials that work in my Office are set out in Dod's Civil Service Companion...Details are also available on the No. 10 website.

Written Answers, Wednesday, 5 May 2006

Norman Baker (Lewes, Liberal Democrat)

To ask the Prime Minister when he plans to issue an updated version of the 28 April 2004 organogram of the No. 10 organisation.

Tony Blair (Prime Minister)

I have nothing further to add to the answer I gave to the Hon. Member on 18 April 2006.

Source: adapted from Hansard.

As of June 2006, therefore, the closest we had was the summary provided in the CO's 2005 Departmental Report (see Box 3.4) and the list of key personnel given on the No. 10 website (see Box 3.5).

Box 3.4

Elements of the Prime Minister's Office, 2005

The Prime Minister's Office, No. 10, works with the Cabinet Office to provide central direction for the development, implementation and presentation of government policy. No. 10 is staffed by a mixture of civil servants and special advisors and headed by a chief of staff. There are a number of different units within No. 10:

● The No. 10 **Policy Directorate** provides advice to the prime minister on domestic and economic policy issues, conveying his views on issues to departments and

---

> ## Box 3.4 (continued)
>
> ensuring follow-up as required. The directorate works closely with ministers, special advisors and officials in other departments. The **Parliamentary Section** handles all parliamentary affairs for the prime minister.
>
> - The **European and Foreign Policy Advisors' Office** provides advice and support to the prime minister on all European Union (EU) business and foreign affairs. It is supported by the European and Defence and Overseas Secretariats in the Cabinet Office.
> - The **Events and Visits Office** manages all visits between the prime minister and overseas heads of government.
> - All the prime minister's communications are issued from No. 10 — the strategy is devised and coordinated by the **Strategic Communications Unit**. The No. 10 **Press Office** handles day-to-day contact with the media. The **Corporate Communications Division** is responsible for all forms of communication directly to and from the public.
> - The **Honours and Appointments** sections at No. 10 support the prime minister in his constitutional role of advising the queen on honours and Crown appointments.
> - Underpinning all responsibilities is the administrative support provided by the team of **duty clerks** and **Garden Room staff**, who work a range of shifts to provide a 24 hours a day, 7 days a week service throughout the year. The **Operations** team provides corporate support for the whole of No. 10 including facilities management, security, IT and telecommunications, finance and human resources.
>
> Source: adapted from Cabinet Office, *Departmental Report 2005*.

> ## Box 3.5
> ### Key No. 10 staff, June 2006
>
> | | |
> |---|---|
> | Jonathan Powel | Chief of Staff |
> | Liz Lloyd | Deputy Chief of Staff |
> | Ivan Rogers | Principal Private Secretary |
> | David Hil | Director of Communications |
> | Jo Gibbons | Director of Events, Visits and Scheduling |
> | John McTernan | Director of Political Operations |
> | David Bennett | Head of Policy Directorate |
> | Matthew Taylor | Chief Advisor on Strategy |
> | Ruth Turner | Director of Government Relations |
>
> Source: www.pm.gov.uk.

Prime ministerial control of government bodies

How much control does the prime minister have over bodies such as the Cabinet Office and the Prime Minister's Office? Even as early as April 2000, R. A. W. Rhodes was happy to conclude that 'No. 10 is omnipresent in [all] serious policy reviews'. Similarly, even the CO's own 2002 spending review held that its 'Objective 1' was 'to support the Prime Minister in leading the Government'. This sense that the PMO and the CO have become tools of prime ministerial control has resulted from a number of factors.

First, and most obviously, the cabinet secretary (the head of the CO) is appointed by and directly answerable to the premier, as are the various ministers who work in the office (see Box 3.6). It is surely no coincidence, for example, that the ministers serving in the CO in June 2006 were all regarded as being fairly loyal to the prime minister. Armstrong was previously the chief whip, and McFadden and Miliband had both been senior special advisors before the 2005 general election.

Box 3.6

Cabinet Office ministers, June 2006

Hilary Armstrong	Minister for the Cabinet Office
Hazel Blears	Minister without Portfolio
Pat McFadden	Parliamentary Secretary
Ed Miliband	Parliamentary Secretary

Second, the period after 2001 saw the creation of a number of key CO units which were either also part of the PMO, or at least headed by individuals holding parallel positions in the PMO. The prime minister's Delivery Unit and the Strategy Unit (both created in 2001), for example, would now appear in organograms for both the CO and the PMO. Similarly, the head of the European Secretariat (CO) has commonly been the prime minister's European policy advisor (PMO), just as the head of the Defence and Overseas Secretariat (CO) has often taken on a role as the prime minister's foreign policy advisor (PMO).

This fusion of the CO with the PMO is a key development for those who have hailed the emergence of a Prime Minister's Department. It is, however, impossible to appreciate fully the prime minister's control of the core executive without touching on the part played by special advisors since 1997.

Special advisors

Has the increase in number and influence of special advisors contributed to the notion that we have a UK West Wing? In the 1980s, key players such as Tony Benn had claimed that the civil service had an inbuilt conservative bias that made it unwilling to support the work of successive Labour ministers. When Labour was returned to office in 1997, therefore, it was keen to avoid the kind of administrative gridlock that had plagued some earlier Labour administrations. It was this desire that drove the reorganisation of the CO and the PMO outlined above. At the same time, the twin focus on 'strategy' and 'delivery' inevitably involved a willingness to put political appointees — as opposed to career civil servants — in key positions.

Though such special advisors (see Box 3.7) and also other unpaid advisors (see Box 3.8) had existed before 1997, with figures such as Margaret Thatcher's press secretary Bernard Ingham and her economics advisor Sir Alan Walters to the fore, they were relatively few (e.g. only five in 1990). By convention, they were also located only in the prime minister's Policy Unit or in the Political Office, with career civil servants filling the other key positions. In the wake of Labour's 1997 general election victory, however, the number of bodies in which such individuals served, the overall number of special advisors in post, and the power and influence that they possessed over those around them — both regular civil servants and, in some cases, even ministers — increased significantly.

Box 3.7

Special advisors

Definitions
- Special advisors are civil servants, paid for by taxpayers.
- Unlike most regular (i.e. career) civil servants, however, they are not bound by the traditional civil service principles of impartiality, anonymity and permanence.

Types
- Policy advisors.
- Media liaison advisors (often referred to as 'spin doctors').

Roles
- To make the government less reliant on the work of the civil service.
- To help the prime minister keep up to date with often far better staffed and resourced government departments.
- To communicate 'the message' effectively to the broader public and ensure that ministers stay 'on message'.

> **Box 3.8**
> **Paid and unpaid advisors**
>
> Though they have an increasingly political role, most of those working within the CO and the PMO are civil servants, paid for through tax revenues.
>
> One or two are paid for by the party in office: for example, in 2006 John McTernan's salary as Director of Political Operations was paid for by the Labour Party.
>
> There are also unpaid advisors. Lord Birt, the former BBC director general, was brought in as unpaid advisor on crime in July 2000 before becoming the strategy advisor to the prime minister in October 2001. In this post Birt was charged with the task of bringing 'blue skies thinking' to a wide range of areas.

Reach

The convention by which special advisors worked only in the prime minister's Policy Unit or the Political Office was abandoned. Consequently, such individuals were appointed both to the new bodies created after 1997, and also to those other bodies that had previously been considered solely the domain of career civil servants.

Numbers

Though each cabinet minister can appoint two special advisors, those appointed directly by and for the prime minister are of particular interest in the context of our efforts to distinguish a UK 'West Wing'. In opposition, Tony Blair had a personal staff of around 20 individuals. In government, many of these figures took on roles as special advisors within the No. 10 machine; 25 such individuals were in post in 2005.

Powers and status

The close working relationship that many special advisors had with the prime minister obviously lent them a degree of authority. In addition, an Order in Council gave up to three politically appointed advisors far-reaching executive powers to give instructions to regular civil servants. This superseded the 1979 order that had allowed them merely to advise. Thus, figures such as Blair's press secretary (later Director of Communications), Alastair Campbell, and his chief of staff, Jonathon Powell, became major players. Though the criticisms levelled at the work of such advisors in the Wicks Report, the Hutton Inquiry and the Phillis Report (see Box 3.9) resulted in the Director of Communications losing his Order in Council powers, it is significant that the chief of staff retained them.

Alastair Campbell (left), with Tony Blair, in his role as press secretary

---

Box 3.9

Special advisors 'in the dock'

Wicks Report, 2003

The ninth report of the Committee on Standards in Public Life, chaired by Sir Nigel Wicks, articulated public concerns over the role and accountability of staff within the Prime Minister's Office, specifically in the area of government communications.

Hutton Inquiry, 2003

Lord Hutton was given the task of investigating the circumstances surrounding the apparent suicide of Dr David Kelly, a senior scientific advisor to the government who had been involved in assessing the threat posed by weapons of mass destruction prior to the joint US/UK invasion of Iraq.

Though many felt that the inquiry was too limited, both in its remit and in its findings, the evidence given during hearings added to calls for regulation of special advisors.

Phillis Report, 2003

The interim report of Robert Phillis's Review of Government Communications high-lighted the breakdown of trust between government, the media and the general public. Phillis's recommendations, which included strengthening the role of the regular civil service in government communications and removing the Director of Communication's Order in Council powers, was accepted by the prime minister.

In addition, it is also worth noting the extent to which the very language used to describe key positions in the CO and the PMO has undergone a process of Americanisation. The list of job titles held by the key PMO staff in 2006 (see Box 3.5), for example, would be immediately familiar to any student of US government and politics.

In short, though the prime minister's special advisors have at times proven more of a liability than a tool (witness Alastair Campbell's declining fortunes after 2002 and his subsequent departure), such figures have clearly given the premier another means by which he can keep tabs on rivals and drive his own policy agenda forward.

Physical relocation of government offices

Accompanying the changes in organisation and staffing at the centre of government has been a physical relocation of many of the bodies involved. Though the CO has traditionally been based at 70 Whitehall, directly adjacent to Downing Street, the second phase of reorganisation in 2001 saw the relocation of the staff from a further 17 former CO buildings to new accommodation in Downing Street.

This expansion — facilitated in part at least by the annexation of the former official residence of the chief whip at No. 12 Downing Street — represents a further step on the road to what might be called a UK 'West Wing'.

Conclusion

The period between 1997 and 2006 witnessed a series of changes that made moot the age-old debate over whether or not the UK needed a Prime Minister's Department. The changes summarised in Box 3.10 attest to the fact that we now have a Prime Minister's Department — a UK 'West Wing' — in all but name.

Box 3.10

Chapter summary

- There has been a massive expansion in the number of bodies working within the Cabinet Office and the Prime Minister's Office.
- Most of these bodies are now directly answerable to the prime minister.

Box 3.10 (continued)

- There has been a fusion of the PMO and the CO.
- Those civil servants working in these bodies as special advisors are now most often political appointees employed on short-term contracts, as opposed to career civil servants.
- The key staff in the 'Prime Minister's Department' are located within easy walking distance of one another; most work in Downing Street itself.

Task 3.1

(a) Explain the difference between *career civil servants* and *special advisors*.
(b) Briefly outline the arguments for and against the greater use of special advisors.

Guidance

(a) Remember, you need clear definitions, appropriate examples and awareness of the debate. It might be helpful to consider the traditional civil service principles of anonymity, impartiality and permanence as a way into this question. If you can, try to identify similarities as well as differences.

(b) Most commentators choose to characterise the rise of the special advisor as being a wholly bad thing, not least as a result of the way in which the presence of such individuals appears to undermine the core principles of the civil service. However, it is important to be able to see the other side of the argument. Think in terms of coordinating government activities and overcoming the supposed intransigence and inertia present in the regular civil service, as characterised by Sir Humphrey in *Yes Minister*.

Task 3.2

(a) In what respects have changes in the structure and organisation of the Cabinet Office and the Prime Minister's Office led to the creation of a *de facto* Prime Minister's Department or UK 'West Wing'?
(b) Should such developments be seen as a 'good' or a 'bad' thing?

Guidance

(a) You should treat this as a traditional essay question. When answering such questions, you need to adopt a structured and systematic approach. Identify three or four major areas that you intend to address in your essay (you could take the four factors identified at the start of this chapter, for example) and then deal with each area in turn in a single paragraph of between one-third and one-half of a side of A4.

Task 3.2 (continued)

(b) As with Task 3.1, question (a), you need to think about the positive aspects of such developments as well as the negative connotations. In some respects, the emergence of a UK 'West Wing' has been a necessary response to the changing political context, nationally and internationally. Though the primary focus of this task is the material provided in this chapter, it might also be helpful to look at Chapter 5, which puts many of these developments into their proper context.

Further reading

- Barberis, P. and Carr, F. (2000) 'Executive control and governance under Tony Blair', *Talking Politics*, vol. 12, no. 3.
- Burnham, J. and Jones, G. (2000) 'Advising the prime minister, 1868–1997', *Talking Politics*, vol. 12, no. 2.
- Jones, A. (2002) 'Special advisors and the demise of Sir Humphrey?', *Talking Politics*, vol. 15, no. 1.
- Kavanagh, D. (2000) 'The power behind the prime minister', *Talking Politics*, vol. 12, no. 3.
- Turner, A. (2003) 'Is there a Prime Minister's Department?', *Politics Review*, vol. 12, no. 3.

Why have prime minister–cabinet relations provoked so much debate?

In Chapters 1 and 2 we examined the extent to which changes in the nature and scope of prime ministerial power have allowed the modern premier a far greater degree of freedom than that afforded to many of his predecessors. Similarly, in Chapter 3, we examined the way in which structural changes at the heart of the core executive — in particular, the growth of the Cabinet Office and the Prime Minister's Office — have strengthened the prime minister's control at the centre.

Such developments have, in themselves, clearly contributed to the ongoing debate over prime minister–cabinet relations. There are, however, a number of other factors that have fed into this debate. In this chapter, we will address the question of why prime minister–cabinet relations have provoked so much debate by putting those factors already identified into their proper context. In so doing we will provide a link between our early consideration of prime ministerial power and the discussion of the cabinet which will follow in Chapter 5.

Our discussion will focus on four overlapping and interconnected factors, each of which can be said to have contributed in some way to keeping prime minister–cabinet relations in the public eye:

1 constitutional opacity and ambiguity
2 constitutional importance
3 memoirs and 'the bastards' on the inside
4 the rise of a less deferential, 24-hour mass media

Constitutional opacity and ambiguity

How has the opacity and ambiguity of the UK constitution contributed to the debate over prime minister–cabinet relations? The fact that the UK lacks a clearly codified constitution has, as we have seen, contributed to a degree of opacity and ambiguity surrounding the respective roles and powers of the prime minister and cabinet. Though it is possible to draw parallels between the UK and US cabinets — in the sense that neither has a clearly defined constitutional role — things are a good deal clearer in the USA. This results from the fact that the US Constitution vests sole executive power in the hands of the president. Indeed, the US Constitution does not mention the cabinet by name. Neither does it give any indication that the president is under an obligation to meet with the heads of executive departments collectively; only that he or she 'may require the opinion, in writing, of the principal Officer in each of the executive Departments' (Article 2, section 2). Thus, a president elected directly rather than as part of a government team is free to use the cabinet as he or she chooses.

In the UK, things are somewhat different. The modern cabinet emerged from parliament in the late seventeenth and early eighteenth centuries as a link between the executive part of government and the legislature. The prime minister, in turn, emerged from the cabinet under the Hanoverians, as the monarch withdrew from the day-to-day business of government. Thus, the cabinet was, as Bagehot put it, the 'efficient secret' of the English constitution (see Box 4.1), and the prime minister was merely *primus inter pares* — first among equals.

Box 4.1

The Bagehotian view of cabinet

'The cabinet, in a word, is a board of control chosen by the legislature, out of persons whom it trusts and knows, to rule the nation…A cabinet is a combining committee — a hyphen which joins, a buckle which fastens, the legislative part of the state to the executive part of the state. In its origin it belongs to the one, in its functions it belongs to the other.'

Source: Walter Bagehot, *The English Constitution* (1867)

The prime minister is not directly elected as chief executive, neither are his or her ministers directly elected to serve in the government. Rather, prime minister and cabinet are drawn from the majority party in the Commons and depend in large part on the support of that party. In addition, prime ministers and their cabinet colleagues often share a political apprenticeship and it is widely accepted that they come to power as a team — in the first instance, at least. Such realities have resulted in opacity and ambiguity in the relations between prime minister and cabinet, and it is this in turn that is at the root of the ongoing controversy over prime minister–cabinet relations (see Box 4.2).

Constitutional importance

Running parallel to the constitutional opacity and ambiguity that is at the heart of much of the contemporary debate regarding prime minister–cabinet relations is a second root cause: the issue of constitutional importance. Put simply, there is a debate over the relative powers of the prime minister because 'it matters'. In an age increasingly concerned with issues of power and accountability, it is inevitable that attention will focus on the question of precisely where decisions are made within the UK system. With the government, more often than not, in command of a workable Commons majority, and the Lords subject to limitations of statute and convention, observers will inevitably focus on how decisions are made within the core executive (see Box 4.3). This, as we discussed above, is far different from the situation in the USA where — for the same reason — attention is focused not on the relations between president and cabinet but on the dynamic of the relationship between president and Congress.

The prime minister's exercise of the royal prerogative in areas of patronage and foreign policy is particularly important in this respect. Whereas such powers were once accepted, almost without question, they are now subject to scrutiny both by the media, as we will see towards the end of this chapter, and by parliament, as we saw in Chapter 2. The controversy surrounding appointments to the Lords in 2006 provides a useful illustration of the way in which the prime minister's use of patronage has prompted debate. Though Tony Blair would certainly not be the first prime minister to have used ennoblement as a reward for political and financial support, the extent to which the loans to the Labour Party had been organised without the knowledge even of the party's treasurer, Jack Dromey, or other senior cabinet colleagues, further fuelled the debate over prime ministerial power. The public reaction to the scandal was similarly revealing. In a survey for the *Sunday Telegraph* (21 May 2006), 53% of voters believed that the prime minister should be prosecuted if the Labour Party was found to have acted illegally over the loans for peerages affair.

The precise relationship between the prime minister, the cabinet and the legislature in the field of foreign affairs has also prompted considerable debate in recent years. In the kind of 'shrinking world' identified by Richard Rose in his 2001 book, *The Prime Minister in a Shrinking World*, the prime minister's ability to wage war and negotiate binding international agreements, without having to secure the approval of either cabinet colleagues or the legislature, is clearly contentious. Though such prerogative powers are hardly recent additions to the premier's armoury, therefore, they have increasingly been seen as anachronistic, in the same way that the presence of hereditary peers in the Lords became untenable as the twentieth century came to a close. Whereas the hereditaries were removed more due to the sense of anachronism than as a result of their own performance, however, the debate over prime minister–cabinet relations has been further fuelled by the behaviour of recent incumbents. The approach of Richard Rose's 'new style of television-age prime ministers' (see Chapter 2), Thatcher, Major and Blair, has certainly heightened the debate over the distribution of power at the centre. Thatcher and Blair's use of patronage, their approach to cabinet and their man-management style have clearly fed into the debate over prime minister–cabinet relations, as did the difficulties faced by John Major in managing his cabinet colleagues following Thatcher's departure in 1990.

Memoirs and 'the bastards' on the inside

As we saw in Box 4.2, a lot of the debate surrounding the relative status and power of prime minister and cabinet inevitably results from what we can glean from 'insiders talking about an insiders' system'. With the cabinet being something of a closed shop, much of what we know filters down to us through the memoirs of those no longer in cabinet, unattributed leaks from those currently serving in high office, from the media (see below) or — more often — through a combination of the three.

Memoirs and diaries have done a great deal to stimulate the debate surrounding prime minister–cabinet relations. The observations of former Labour ministers of the 1970s such as Richard Crossman and Tony Benn (see Box 4.4) were certainly at the heart of the debate in the 1980s. In their diaries and other writings, and in their public comments, such individuals charted the rise of **prime ministerial government**. Though academic commentators such as Foley have taken the debate on by heralding the emergence of the presidential prime minister, the contributions of Crossman, Benn et al. have clearly been crucial. Similarly, much of what we know about the way in which Tony Blair has operated as prime minister has stemmed from the recollections of former cabinet members such as Mo Mowlam, whose autobiography, *Momentum*, and the accompanying BBC documentary, *Cabinet Confidential*, made wide-ranging criticisms of Blair's *modus operandi* (see Box 4.5).

Box 4.4
Crossman and Benn

Richard Crossman

Crossman had served in a number of cabinet positions under Labour prime minister Harold Wilson in the 1960s before returning to the back benches in 1970 in order to become editor of the *New Statesman*. Crossman is best remembered for his *Diaries of a Cabinet Minister* (covering three volumes), in which he first raised his concerns over the emergence of prime ministerial government.

Tony Benn

A committed left winger, Benn served in the Labour governments of the 1960s and 1970s under Wilson and later Callaghan. Like Crossman, Benn became a prolific diarist, author of books and articles, and public speaker. He was at the forefront of the Stop the War Campaign in 2003 and a long-term critic of the rise in prime ministerial power.

> Box 4.5
> ## Mo Mowlam on Blair
>
> 'Former cabinet member Mo Mowlam has savaged "presidential" Blair, claiming that
> he "makes decisions with a small coterie of people, advisors…just like the president of
> the United States…He doesn't go back to cabinet", she continued, "he isn't inclusive in
> terms of other cabinet ministers…They [the special advisors] seemed to be operating
> instead of the cabinet."
>
> Ms Mowlam, who stepped down from parliament at the [2001 general] election, also
> confirmed a rift between Mr Blair and Chancellor Gordon Brown, saying the two men
> "aren't working together". "You know there's a battle going on and people support, or
> people go to, one side or the other. I think that is just crippling for government." '
>
> Source: adapted from BBC news (online), 17 November 2001.

Alongside the official memoirs and legitimate observations of those no longer in office, the last two decades have also witnessed a greater tendency for those still serving in cabinet to make their views public — often, though not always, anonymously — through the media. Though such leaks clearly fly in the face of any notion of collective responsibility within cabinet (see Chapter 5), they have greatly contributed to the debate over prime minister–cabinet relations.

This willingness on the part of those inside cabinet to undermine the prime minister by briefing the press was amply illustrated during John Major's time in office (see Box 4.6). Having set himself the task of securing Commons approval for the Maastricht Treaty, the prime minister's efforts were undermined not only by those on the back benches — particularly the 'Whipless Wonders' we spoke of in Chapter 2 — but also by some of his more Eurosceptic cabinet colleagues. Major found himself in an invidious position: was he to leave 'the bastards' in post, ignoring the fact that they were undermining the government; or return them to the back benches, where their rebellion might become open and, therefore, far more dangerous — in the short term, at least? Major opted for the second course of action, though it did him little good in the long term. The recriminations continued up to and beyond John Redwood's abortive party leadership

John Major as prime minister was undermined by those inside cabinet

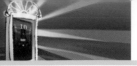

challenge in 1995, and contributed to the sense of infighting and division that helped facilitate Labour's return to office in 1997.

Box 4.6

Major and 'the bastards'

'John Major's rage and frustration with right-wing Tories boiled over this weekend when, in an outburst, he called three of his own cabinet members "bastards". The onslaught against the Eurosceptic ministers, not named, but almost certainly Michael Howard, Peter Lilley and Michael Portillo, came within minutes of the vote of confidence on Friday which kept him in office.

The attack…is on video tape, recorded when he did not know he could still be heard. [On the tape] Mr Major bares his soul. "I could bring in other people [to cabinet]. But where do you think most of this poison is coming from? From the dispossessed and the never possessed. You can think of ex-ministers who are going around causing all sorts of trouble. We don't want another three more of the bastards out there. What's Lyndon Johnson's maxim?" [It's probably better to have the son-of-a-bitch inside the tent pissing out than outside the tent pissing in].'

Source: adapted from 'Major hits out at cabinet', *Observer*, 25 July 1993.

The years following Labour's second consecutive general election victory in 2001 witnessed similar scenes. Robin Cook, who had been switched — some argued, demoted — from the post of foreign secretary to that of leader of the Commons in 2001, resigned from the cabinet in 2003 over the proposed military intervention in Iraq. Clare Short, as we saw in Chapter 2, initially remained in cabinet despite the fact that she had publicly criticised the invasion. On an issue that the prime minister had claimed was a judgement call — even an issue of confidence — Cook and Short both argued that there had been insufficient cabinet discussion of options other than military action. Their open opposition and, ultimately, their resignations certainly contributed to the debate over prime minister–cabinet relations at the time. Similarly, press reports that some of those in cabinet were unhappy with the prime minister's agenda for education reform in 2006 (see Box 4.7) were also evidence of the way in which the activities of those in office can fuel the longstanding debate over relations at the centre.

Though such backbiting would have always interested academics and those inside the 'Westminster village', it would have had little impact — in the broader sense — were it not for the activities of the mass media. It is they who feed their audience's appetite for information about those in high office and, in some cases perhaps, create an appetite where none previously existed.

> **Box 4.7**
>
> **Unease over education reforms**
>
> 'Ruth Kelly yesterday poured petrol on the flames of protest over the government's education reforms, telling critics, including the former Labour leader Neil Kinnock and former education secretary Estelle Morris, that they "don't understand" the plans.
>
> [Morris] is one of the highest-profile members of a campaign that now extends across the parliamentary Labour party and the cabinet. John Prescott, Patricia Hewitt and the international development secretary, Hilary Benn, are among those at the top of government unhappy at the proposals. Criticism lower down the ranks is more explicit, with 90 Labour MPs supporting the alternative white paper.'
>
> Source: adapted from the *Guardian*, 21 January 2006.

The rise of the modern mass media

The last two decades have witnessed a decline in the kind of deference that was once — alongside homogeneity and consensus — said to be a defining characteristic of UK political culture (see Box 4.8). Key to this decline in deference has been the rise of the modern mass media. Put simply, it is argued that media more willing to expose the inner workings of government to public scrutiny have contributed to the development of a citizenry more aware of the vagaries of politics and less willing to allow politicians to get on with the business of government. This clearly has a bearing on our consideration of the factors that have fed into the debate over prime minister–cabinet relations. By bringing the tensions that have always existed within cabinet into the public eye, the media have allowed for the kind of public debate that might previously have involved only those 'insiders' identified by Hennessey in Box 4.2.

> **Box 4.8**
>
> **Political culture**
>
> '[Political culture consists of] the opinions, attitudes and beliefs which shape political behaviour. A country's political culture consists of the whole citizenry's collective attitudes to the political system and their role in it.'
>
> Source: Coxall, B. and Robins, L. (1998) *Contemporary British Politics*, Macmillan.

Parallel to this decline in media deference has been a massive expansion in the range and volume of media output. The early years of the twenty-first century have seen the emergence of a genuinely 24-hour media machine,

encompassing television (analogue and digital, terrestrial and satellite), radio, newspaper and magazines, and the internet. The sheer quantity of air-time, newsprint and web-space that must be filled on a daily basis creates a demand for content that inevitably outstrips the supply of genuine news. The result of this overcapacity is increased time afforded to comment, informed debate and/or speculation. Whereas such material might once have been confined to newspaper editorials and late-night current affairs programmes, it has increasingly colonised the space formerly devoted to more mainstream 'news' stories. In this context, prime minister–cabinet relations provide an ever-present topic for debate. Though such debates will obviously be more intense where the behaviour of those in office warrants more detailed consideration, such behaviour or other incident is certainly not a prerequisite for media speculation.

This truth can be amply illustrated by a consideration of the media coverage of Tony Blair's political future, both in advance of and following the 2005 general election. Prior to the poll, media speculation centring on when the prime minister might step down and who might replace him as Labour leader eventually resulted in Blair going public on his decision not to lead the party into a fourth successive general election. After the general election of 2005, the media switched their focus on to the question of precisely when the prime minister would step down; when he would name the date. This media debate went on well into 2006 (see Box 4.9).

Box 4.9

Waiting for Blair to 'name the date'

'Hilary Benn, the International Development Secretary, has been forced to disown his parliamentary aide after he called on Tony Blair to stand aside rapidly in favour of Gordon Brown. Ashok Kumar, Parliamentary Private Secretary to Mr Benn, is the first — albeit junior — government member to call on Mr Blair to quit.

Mr Benn said: "The prime minister has made it clear that he will decide when he will stand down and I think it would be better if we all got on with the business of government."

Source: adapted from 'Minister disowns aide over "Blair must stand down" claim', the *Guardian*, 30 March 2006.

The intensity of the media speculation surrounding the time of Blair's departure and the question of who should succeed him was again apparent in the wake of Deputy Prime Minister John Prescott's fall from grace in May 2006. First, it was reported that Prescott had retained the post of deputy education secretary, only because a contest for the job of deputy would put pressure on

Blair to step down, thereby precipitating a simultaneous election for leader. Second, and despite the fact that Prescott had survived the reshuffle, several newspapers ran with a list of candidates who might replace him. When the newly installed education secretary Alan Johnson publicly stated his intention to run for the job of deputy prime minister, should it become available, some commentators speculated that he might in fact prove a worthy rival to Gordon Brown for the job of prime minister. Throughout this time, figures 'close to the chancellor' were heard on a regular basis, urging Blair to 'name a date' for his departure and championing the merits of their man (see Box 4.10).

Gordon Brown

Box 4.10

Brownites keep up the pressure

'Tony Blair came under carefully choreographed public and private pressure from Gordon Brown's closest supporters yesterday to set out the timetable for his departure in the wake of dire local election results.

In an escalation of the power struggle between New Labour's two creators, Andrew Smith, a former cabinet minister and an ally of Mr Brown, identified Mr Blair as the problem on the doorstep in the elections.'

Source: adapted from 'Plotters move to oust Blair', the *Guardian*, 6 May 2006.

Conclusion

Though the debate over prime minister–cabinet relations is, as we have seen, rooted in the uncertainty that has resulted from the UK's uncodified constitution, it has clearly intensified in recent years as a result of a number of interconnected factors. Of these, the role of the modern media has proven most crucial. This is one of the themes that we will explore further in Chapter 6, when we tackle the question of whether or not the UK now has presidential government. First, however, we need to examine the state of the cabinet at the start of the twenty-first century.

Task 4.1

(a) Can we really trust the memoirs of former cabinet ministers?

(b) Study Box 4.6. John Major was unaware that his 'off-air' comments were still being recorded. It is unlikely that he would have made such remarks 'on the record'. Write one paragraph arguing that this kind of media exposé is 'good' for democracy, and another arguing that it is 'bad'.

Guidance

(a) It is always best to consider the reliability of any written source in terms of the situation and purpose of the author in question. When we talk about the 'situation' we are really asking whether or not the author is in a position to know about the things he or she is talking about and whether he or she is in a position to tell us. Former cabinet members are clearly in a position to know, though the doctrine of collective responsibility and the Radcliffe rules (see Chapter 5, Box 5.10) were supposed to limit their freedom to speak out. When questioning the 'purpose' of an author, we are considering the reasons why he or she has chosen to commit his or her thoughts to paper. An author who is motivated primarily by financial gain or by a desire for revenge is less likely to give a reliable account of his or her experiences in government.

(b) When arguing that such revelations are 'good' for democracy, it might be helpful to think in terms of 'public interest' and the benefits of allowing voters to make 'informed choices' at the next election. When arguing that such media coverage is 'bad' for democracy, you might consider the way in which reports like this can destabilise the government and feed into a broader cynicism regarding politicians and the world in which they operate.

Further reading

- McNaughton, N. (2002) 'Prime ministerial government', *Talking Politics*, vol. 15, no. 1.
- Thomas, G. (2002) 'The prime minister and cabinet', *Politics Review*, vol. 11, no. 4.

Chapter 5

Whatever happened to the cabinet?

As we saw in Chapter 4, the debate over prime minister–cabinet relations has intensified in recent years as a result of a number of overlapping and interconnected developments. Whereas the cabinet was once seen as the supreme decision-making committee of government, contemporary academic discussion of the cabinet more often centres on the twin themes of disempowerment and decline.

This stands in stark contrast to the picture painted by Walter Bagehot in his seminal 1867 work, *The English Constitution*. For Bagehot, the cabinet was the 'efficient' centre of government (see Box 5.1), despite the fact that, even in the nineteenth century, the role of the premier was taking on more constitutional significance.

Box 5.1

The 'dignified' and 'efficient' elements of the constitution

In his 1867 work, *The English Constitution*, Walter Bagehot drew a distinction between the 'dignified' and 'efficient' elements of the constitution.

Dignified elements were 'those which excite and preserve the reverence of the population' but 'have little real power'. Efficient elements were 'those by which, in fact, it rules'.

For Bagehot, the cabinet was the key efficient element.

The Bagehotian view of cabinet persisted, in large part, into the modern era. Indeed, even for most of the twentieth century, the cabinet was said to be a collegiate body, whose collectivity was characterised by two key mutually supporting facets:

1 Cabinet was a collective decision-making body: that is, it was the place where decisions over the direction and scope of policy were debated and then decided collectively.
2 Cabinet operated under the doctrine of collective responsibility. It was a place where those present agreed to stand by the decisions made in closed session, regardless of whether or not they themselves had personally supported the agreed line (see Box 5.2).

> ## Box 5.2
> ## The cabinet as a 'collective body'
>
> 'Decisions reached by the Cabinet or Ministerial Committees are binding on all members of the Government...Collective responsibility requires that Ministers should be able to express their views frankly in the expectation that they can argue freely in private while maintaining a united front when decisions have been reached. This in turn requires that the privacy of opinions expressed in Cabinet and Ministerial Committees should be maintained.'
>
> Source: *Ministerial Code: A Code of Conduct and Guidance on Procedures for Ministers*, June 2001 (paragraphs 16 and 17).

This then was the basis of what became known as 'cabinet government'. In this chapter we will examine the notion of cabinet government briefly, before moving on to identify five factors that can be said to have contributed to its decline. In so doing we will pave the way for our discussion of 'the British presidency' in Chapter 6.

A Labour cabinet meeting

What is cabinet government?

In the UK, the term 'cabinet government' refers to the way in which executive power was traditionally said to rest with cabinet, as a collective decision-making body (see Box 5.2). This contrasts markedly with the situation in the USA, where, as we saw in Chapter 4, sole executive power is vested in the hands of an independently elected chief executive: the president.

Though the modern cabinet is still said to perform the three roles identified in Box 5.3, the reality is clearly somewhat different. Specifically, though the modern cabinet still has a part to play with respect to interdepartmental coordination, its significance in the areas of decision making and strategic planning has, it is argued, diminished significantly. Though this diminution of cabinet has often been seen in the context of the parallel growth in the scope and nature of the powers of the prime minister, this is — as we will see — only part of the picture.

> Box 5.3
> **The roles of cabinet**
>
> **1** decision making
> **2** interdepartmental coordination
> **3** strategic planning

In answering the question posed in the title of this chapter, we will, therefore, need to identify and address a number of interwoven factors:

- the increase in the scope and complexity of government activity
- the emergence and subsequent rise of cabinet committees
- the tendency towards the use of bilateral meetings and other less formal arrangements over full cabinet meetings
- the increase in the authority and status afforded to the prime minister
- the behaviour of those serving in cabinet

The scope and complexity of government

How has the increase in the scope and complexity of government contributed to a diminution of cabinet power? The years since Bagehot made his observations on the role played by cabinet have witnessed massive changes, both in the scope and scale of government activity and in its complexity.

- **Scope and scale.** The state is actively involved in far more aspects of our everyday lives than was the case in the late nineteenth century. In Bagehot's time, the government's approach was still — more often than not — best summed up in the phrase *laissez faire* (let it be). A move towards greater state intervention, particularly in the areas of welfare provision and economic management, has inevitably resulted in far 'bigger' government.
- **Complexity.** The growth in the work of government has not simply been quantitative (i.e. greater volume) but also qualitative. Modern government involves a degree of technical complexity that would have been unimaginable in the Bagehotian era.

Such realities were apparent even in 1916 (see Box 5.4), when the first cabinet secretary, Maurice Hankey, introduced a series of administrative reforms aimed at helping the government to cope with the pressures brought by the UK's involvement in the First World War. Since Hankey's time, however, the scale and complexity of government has grown further, not least with the emergence of the welfare state and the UK's membership of the European Union. The cumulative effect of such developments has been to render the Bagehotian notion of a single, supreme governing committee untenable. Put simply, the sheer volume of work, allied with its complexity, has forced the process of government to spread beyond a single body of around 23 generalists (see Box 5.5).

Box 5.4

Maurice Hankey and the emergence of the modern cabinet

Hankey was appointed secretary to the War Cabinet in 1916, when David Lloyd George replaced Herbert Asquith as prime minister. Hankey's reputation for efficiency and organisation meant that he was retained as the first true cabinet secretary when full cabinet was restored in 1919.

Hankey was responsible for a number of key developments in the structure and organisation of cabinet:

- The office of cabinet secretary was created alongside a new Cabinet Secretariat.
- A system of cabinet committees was established.
- Formal minutes of cabinet meetings were kept and circulated, allowing a record to be kept of all that was discussed and — more importantly, perhaps — agreed in cabinet.

Box 5.5

Cabinet sidelined

'It was no longer feasible to expect the cabinet to deliberate and to decide upon the weighty matters of the day. It had become a panel providing political clearance and official sanction for decisions taken elsewhere.'

Source: Foley, M. (1993) *The Rise of the British Presidency*, Manchester University Press.

Such developments have, in turn, resulted in the emergence of a number of other bodies and practices:

- **Cabinet committees.** Though cabinet committees originated with the changes made by Hankey at the time of the First World War (see Box 5.4), the number of committees and the subcommittees that operate below them has proliferated in recent years. Cabinet committees are, as we will see later in the chapter, crucial to the way in which modern government works. First, they address the issues of workload associated with the increasing scope and size of government. Second, they address issues of specialism and complexity by bringing together smaller groups of ministers who can look at specific areas in more detail.

- **Bilaterals and other informal groupings.** Though the use of bilaterals is, as we have seen, often associated with the prime minister's efforts to 'divide and rule' in cabinet, meetings between the premier and a single minister clearly make a good deal of sense where the complexity, or more often the specialised nature, of the issue makes early discussion among a committee of 23 generalists pointless. Similarly, other informal groupings — such as the 'kitchen cabinets' or 'war cabinets' that have operated at certain points during the modern era — may also serve to provide a more appropriate forum for discussion than full cabinet meetings.

- **Changes in departments.** The increasing volume and complexity of the work done in government has inevitably had consequences for the way in which departments operate. First, and most significantly, it has meant that cabinet-level ministers now have to devote the bulk of their time to keeping abreast of developments within their own portfolio and to managing those for whom they are responsible. The series of scandals that engulfed the Home Office in 2006, eventually resulting in the departure of the then home secretary Charles Clarke, demonstrated just how difficult it is to keep a grip on a large ministry. Though some of the burden has been lifted as a result of the process of agencification — hiving off some aspects of departmental delivery to free-standing agencies, which began under Margaret Thatcher — the job of managing one's own department remains a massive one. As a result, it could be argued that the cabinet will inevitably become a less collegiate body: because ministers are so busy trying to keep a grip on their own department that they are less able and less inclined to speak out on areas outside their remit.

- **The rise of the Cabinet Office and Prime Minister's Office.** As we saw in Chapter 3, the blend of ministers, special advisors and career civil servants within such bodies — and the extent to which those involved are directly answerable to the prime minister — has clearly led to the diminution in the role of full cabinet meetings in the areas of departmental coordination, strategic planning and policy delivery.

The rise of cabinet committees

How has the rise of cabinet committees affected the role of the cabinet itself? As we have seen, cabinet committees first emerged at the time of the First World War as a means of relieving the workload on the cabinet and providing more focused consideration of specific areas of policy. Since that time, such committees and their associated subcommittees have proliferated (see Box 5.6 and Table 5.1).

> **Box 5.6**
>
> ## Different types of cabinet committee
>
> **Standing committees**
> Permanent bodies, organised into categories such as foreign and defence policy, domestic/ home affairs and economic policy, e.g. the Energy and the Environment Committee (EE).
>
> **Ad hoc/miscellaneous committees**
> Set up to deal with specific issues or concerns, e.g. the Olympics Committee (MISC 25).

Table 5.1 Cabinet committees and subcommittees, May 2006

Standing committees	
Committee	**Subcommittee**
AntiSocial Behaviour (ASB)	
Asylum and Migration (AM)	
Civil Contingencies (CCC)	
Constitutional Affairs (CA)	CA(EP) Electoral Policy
	CA(FoI) Freedom of Information
	CA(PM) Parliamentary Modernisation
Intelligence Services (CSI)	
Defence and Overseas Policy (DOP)	DOP(IT) International Terrorism
	DOP(IT)(PSR) Protective Security and Resilience
	DOP(I) Iraq
	DOP(CPR) Conflict Prevention and Reconstruction
Domestic Affairs (DA)	DA(AP) Ageing Policy
	DA(CP) Children's Policy
	DA(C) Communities
	DA(L) Legal Affairs
	DA(PH) Public Health

(continued)

Standing committees	
Committee	**Subcommittee**
Economic Affairs, Productivity and Competitiveness (EAPC)	
Energy and the Environment (EE)	EE(SD) Sustainable Development in Government
European Policy (EP)	
European Union Strategy (EUS)	
Housing and Planning (HP)	
Identity Management (IM)	
Legislative Programme (LP)	
Local and Regional Government (LRG)	LRG(P) Local Government Strategy and Performance
National Health Service Reform (HSR)	
Public Services and Public Expenditure (PSX)	PSX(E) Electronic Service Delivery
Public Services Reform (PSR)	
Regulation, Bureaucracy and Risk (RB)	RB(PRA) Panel on Regulatory Accountability RB(I) Inspection
Schools Policy (SR)	
Science and Innovation (SI)	
Serious and Organised Crime and Drugs (SOC)	
Social Exclusion (SE)	
Welfare Reform (WR)	

Ad hoc/miscellaneous committees	
Committee	**Subcommittee**
Restructuring of the European Aerospace and Defence Industry (MISC 5)	
Animal Rights Activists (MISC 13)	
Olympics (MISC 25)	
London (MISC 26)	

(continued)

Ad hoc/miscellaneous committees	
Committee	**Subcommittee**
Efficiency and Relocation (MISC 30)	
Data Sharing (MISC 31)	
Influenza Pandemic Planning (MISC 32)	
Post Office Network (MISC 33)	

Source: Cabinet Office website, 26 June 2006.

A good deal of debate surrounds the issue of whether or not such committees are, on the whole, a 'good' or a 'bad' thing. Those who champion the use of committees argue that they are a necessary means of dealing with the nature of modern government. Critics, in contrast, see the cabinet committees as one of the means by which cabinet has been deliberately circumvented by prime ministers looking to enhance their own control over the direction and pace of policy. Though the way in which such committees are invariably chaired by either the prime minister or other senior ministers chosen by him has provoked controversy, much of the debate necessarily focuses on the status of decisions made within committee. In short, are cabinet committees actually making decisions or are they simply making recommendations to cabinet, where the real decisions are made?

The Ministerial Code, first published in 1992 and amended on a number of occasions since, sheds a good deal of light on this debate (see Box 5.7). What is increasingly clear, both from this document and from the insights of

---

Box 5.7

Cabinet committees and the power of decision making

'The internal process through which a decision has been made, or the level of Committee by which it was taken, should not be disclosed. Decisions reached by the Cabinet or Ministerial Committees are binding on all members of the Government. They are, however, normally announced and explained as the decision of the Minister concerned. On occasions it may be desirable to emphasise the importance of a decision by stating specially that it is the decision of Her Majesty's Government. This, however, is the exception rather than the rule.'

Source: *Ministerial Code: A Code of Conduct and Guidance on Procedures for Ministers*, June 2001 (paragraph 16).

---

insiders, is that the vast bulk of government business is now decided not in cabinet proper, but in committee. Moreover, though many cabinet members will have had no part in the decisions made in committee, they are still bound by the doctrine of collective responsibility to support such decisions. The Ministerial Code's insistence that 'the internal process through which a decision has been made, or the level of Committee by which it was taken, should not be disclosed' (see Box 5.7) should be seen in this context. Public disclosure of precisely where a decision was made might easily provide a means by which the media could drive a wedge between individual cabinet members.

Bilateral meetings and informal groupings of ministers

It is generally argued that the increasing tendency for the prime minister to engage in bilateral and informal meetings with one or more ministers outside of full cabinet meetings has undermined the notion that the cabinet is the key collective decision-making body in the UK government.

It is wise, however, to make one or two salient points regarding such a hypothesis. First, Blair was not the first to operate outside of cabinet meetings. Talk of inner cabinets and kitchen cabinets was common in the press and in academic works long before Labour returned to office in 1997. Second, such meetings actually make a lot of sense in the light of the developments we have already discussed in this chapter.

That said, it is clear that developments in respect of the prime minister's use of extra-cabinet meetings since 1997 have taken the debate to an entirely different level, not simply because of a genuine concern over the manner in which such meetings have been conducted, but because of what it means for the cabinet — our primary concern at this point in our discussion.

In his report of 2004, the former cabinet secretary Lord Butler made a number of general observations regarding the way in which policy had been formulated ahead of the joint US/UK invasion of Iraq (see Box 5.8). Though the Butler Report focused on the failures of intelligence regarding the likely presence of weapons of mass destruction in Iraq, we might easily apply some of his observations to the way in which the core executive has functioned in general since Labour was returned to power in 1997.

> Box 5.8
> **Failings at the heart of government?**
>
> - Government was too informal in its decision-making process, with too little use being made of established cabinet committee machinery.
> - The cabinet secretary had been cut out of the loop through the appointment of a separate security and intelligence coordinator who was directly responsible to the prime minister.
> - Prime ministerial control had been further enhanced by the decision to merge two key posts in the Cabinet Secretariat, those of head of the Defence and Overseas Secretariat and head of the European Secretariat, with the posts of prime minister's advisors on foreign affairs and on European affairs respectively (see Chapter 3).
> - Though policy towards Iraq had been an agenda item at cabinet meetings on 24 occasions in the year before the war, small groups of key ministers, civil servants and the military provided the framework for discussion and decision making in the government as the war drew near.
>
> Source: based on the Butler Report, 14 July 2004, pp. 146–47 (Stationery Office).

Any number of commentators have remarked upon Tony Blair's penchant for 'sofa government', where informal, unminuted bilateral meetings are conducted in the ante-chambers of No. 10. Butler's comments regarding 'small groups of key ministers [and] civil servants' are also familiar in light of the way in which 'ministerial groups' and 'official committees' have emerged in support of the more formalised standing committees in cabinet in recent years (see Box 5.9).

> Box 5.9
> **Ministerial groups and official committees**
>
> **Ministerial groups**
> These are less formalised than standing or ad hoc committees and include some individuals outside of the cabinet alongside selected cabinet ministers. Such groups emerged after 1997 and were supposed to aid the delivery of 'joined-up government'.
>
> **Official committees**
> These consist entirely of civil servants and are chaired by the Cabinet Secretariat. According to the Cabinet Office website, such groups are 'usually arranged ahead of a [Cabinet] Committee meeting [in order] to identify and clarify key issues prior to Ministerial discussion'.

The emergence of the modern prime minister

How has the emergence of the modern prime minister accelerated the decline of cabinet? We identified many of the factors that have led to a growth in prime ministerial power in earlier chapters, and we will be returning to the question of whether or not the UK has presidential government in Chapter 6. That said, it is clearly important to acknowledge the part that the emergence of the modern prime minister has played in the demise of the cabinet as a collective decision-making body.

As we saw in Chapter 4, the debate over the nature and influence of the cabinet is inextricably linked to that surrounding the power of the prime minister, partly due to the way in which the post of prime minister emerged from cabinet in the eighteenth century. Though the debate is often framed in terms of the prime minister 'taking power', or the cabinet 'giving it up', the rebalancing of prime minister–cabinet relations, as we have seen in this chapter, has as much to do with the context (e.g. the increasing complexity of government and the rise of the mass media) as it has to do with personalities. Thus we might see the rise of the prime minister and the decline of cabinet as being the mirror halves of a single process, as opposed to simply 'cause' and 'effect'.

The behaviour of cabinet ministers

Those in cabinet were traditionally expected to operate under the twin doctrines of collective responsibility and individual ministerial responsibility. The former, as we have seen, demands that cabinet ministers publicly stand by those decisions made collectively within cabinet. The latter holds them responsible for the conduct of their departments ('role responsibility') and for their own personal conduct ('personal responsibility'), with the expectation that they will resign in the event that they fail in either sphere. In recent years, both doctrines appear to have been less faithfully adhered to.

Whatever happened to collective responsibility?

We have already examined the extent to which the demise of collective decision making has inevitably brought into question the doctrine of collective

responsibility within cabinet. It is clearly unreasonable to expect ministers to stand four-square behind a decision that will, in all likelihood, have been arrived at without their direct involvement: in cabinet committee, in bilateral meetings or in other ministerial groups.

In a similar vein, as we saw in Chapter 4, revelations made in memoirs (despite the guidelines set out in the Radcliffe Report of 1976 — see Box 5.10), leaks (e.g. Major's 'bastards') and even open dissent (e.g. Clare Short over Iraq) have served to undermine the notion that cabinet discussions should remain confidential. Though we should acknowledge that Blair was not the first of the 'new media age' prime ministers to suffer open dissent of the type demonstrated by Short (see Box 5.11), the decline in the willingness of cabinet ministers to maintain a united front publicly has clearly gathered pace in recent years.

Box 5.10

The Radcliffe Report, 1976

'Most of the issues [concerning the publication of memoirs and diaries] were aired in the Radcliffe report of 1976 after the Richard Crossman diaries. The Radcliffe rules were intended to protect confidences for 15 years and require former ministers and officials to submit any books, subject to the constraints of not damaging national security, international relations and "confidential relationships of ministers with each other or their officials".

Professor Hennessy argues that voluntary restraints based on a "good chaps" system have broken down and should be replaced by a five-year rule.'

Source: Riddell, P., 'Dear diary, must ensure you don't get in the way of government', *The Times* (online), 18 November 2005.

Box 5.11

Collective responsibility: some failures to resign

'**James Callaghan**, a member of Wilson's cabinet, campaigned against the government's plans to reform the trade unions in 1969.

Keith Joseph and **Margaret Thatcher** did not resign from the Heath government in the early 1970s, even though they opposed Heath's so-called U-turn.

Geoffrey Howe argued for joining the ERM (exchange rate mechanism) in 1989 when it was not government policy.

Michael Portillo made a number of speeches in 1994 that did not appear to be in line with the policies of the Major government.'

Source: Magee, E. and Garnett, M. (2002) 'Is cabinet government dead?', *Politics Review*, vol. 12, no. 1.

Whatever happened to individual ministerial responsibility?

As is the case with collective responsibility, the doctrine of individual ministerial responsibility in both of its traditional forms — role responsibility and personal responsibility — has come under enormous pressure in recent years.

Role responsibility

The idea that ministers should be directly responsible for and, therefore, accountable for all that goes on in their departments (i.e. role responsibility) has been undermined by three broad and interrelated developments:

1 The growth of government activity identified earlier in this chapter has made the task of keeping on top of one's department very challenging indeed.

2 The process of agencification has made it more difficult to require the resignation of ministers where failures occur. The blame is far more likely to fall on the shoulders of the director of the agency in question.

3 The extent to which the prime minister and other leading ministers are willing to interfere in areas of policy that were formerly within the remit of another minister has made it far more difficult for that minister to have ownership of and, therefore, responsibility for the policies in question.

The cumulative result of these three factors has been a marked reluctance of ministers to fall on their own sword, even where their culpability is apparent to all. Thus, whereas Lord Carrington resigned as foreign secretary in 1982, days after the Argentinian invasion of the Falkland Islands, Norman Lamont took a full 8 months to go following 'Black Wednesday' in 1992 and Charles Clarke was similarly reluctant to make way after a series of damaging failures in the Home Office brought his competence in managing the department into question in 2006. Though there were certainly always ministers in decades past who were reluctant to go, and equally those in more recent times who have made speedy exits, these are the exceptions rather than the rule.

Personal responsibility

The last 20 years have seen a marked decline in the observance of the personal element of the doctrine of individual ministerial responsibility. Whereas it was common even under the Conservatives in the 1980s and 1990s to see ministers resigning as a result of personal misdemeanours, such as affairs and other sexual indiscretions (e.g. Cecil Parkinson, David Mellor), few have done so quickly or willingly since 1997, despite the fact that the personal behaviour of figures such as David Blunkett and John Prescott was not so very different from that of those who had stood down a decade or more before.

What is wrong with the modern breed of cabinet minister?

The common theme linking the decline in the observance of each facet of ministerial responsibility and collective responsibility is the reluctance of ministers to go quickly: when they strongly disagree with what is agreed in cabinet (collective responsibility); when they demonstrably fail to discharge their departmental duties (role responsibility); or when they get caught in a 'compromising position' (personal responsibility). With prime ministers often unwilling to push those who refuse to jump — for fear of creating backbench enemies or parading party disunity in the press — such situations now commonly drag on for weeks (see Box 5.12).

David Blunkett who was forced to resign as home secretary in 2004 after a scandal involving speeding up the visa application of his ex-lover's Filipino nanny

---

Box 5.12

Prerequisites for resignation

'The minister must be yielding, his prime minister unbending, his party out for blood.'

Source: Finers, S. E. (1956) 'The individual responsibility of ministers', *Public Administration*, no. 34.

Though it is tempting to place the responsibility for such messy and drawn-out departures firmly at the door of the prime minister, other factors may also have played their part. It could be argued, for example, that the elevation of 'career politicians' to cabinet-level posts has changed the nature of the game. Whereas Conservative ministers of the 1980s, such as Carrington (role responsibility) and Heseltine (collective responsibility), went quickly, we should remember that both men had enjoyed successes outside of politics prior to taking high office: Carrington, a hereditary peer, had served with distinction in the military during the Second World War; Heseltine was a self-made millionn-aire. Some have argued that the kinds of career path followed by many recent cabinet members makes them far less willing to leave office; for it is all that they know. Such a desire to 'climb the greasy pole' may also have a wider bearing on the nature of prime minister–cabinet relations, as it makes the premier's cabinet colleagues far less likely to rock the boat in the normal course of events.

Conclusion

In an article in *Talking Politics* in September 2003, Mark Rathbone adapted Monty Python's famous 'Dead Parrot Sketch' to argue that cabinet government, far from being deceased, had simply been 'stunned', only to wake up and 'give its owner a savage pecking' in 1990. While this metaphor raises some interesting questions regarding the dynamics of the relationship between prime minister and cabinet, it also has its flaws.

First, Margaret Thatcher's fall from grace in 1990 was prompted as much by the electoral fears of long-term Conservative backbenchers as it was by serving cabinet members, those senior colleagues whom she had sent back to the back benches, or those who had returned there of their own volition. Though the drama of Thatcher calling in her cabinet colleagues one by one for their counsel, before announcing her decision to resign, lingers long in the memory, this was more a recognition that the party needed a new face to put before the electorate than it was a more far-reaching reassertion of the traditional roles and powers of cabinet. Similarly, Major's difficulties in cabinet can be attributed to the internecine conflict within the party that followed Thatcher's forced resignation from office, the broader political context between 1990 and 1997, and his own limitations.

Second, it is wrong to see the balance of power between prime minister and cabinet in the form of a pendulum, which may swing one way or the other but will, in time, return to a point of equilibrium. The reality is that the fundamental changes in the scope and complexity of government outlined earlier in this chapter have permanently altered the very nature of cabinet. The cabinet itself is not, therefore, 'dead', neither is it 'resting'; it has simply become a good deal more 'dignified' with age (see Box 5.13).

Box 5.13

The death of cabinet government?

'Cabinet today is a dignified rather than efficient part of the constitution, as new-style prime ministers have decided that lengthy discussions among twenty MPs with diverse views and departmental responsibilities are a waste of time. In a complementary way, ministers prefer to get on with their own departmental responsibilities rather than listen to discussions about matters that are decided over their heads or behind their backs.'

Source: Rose, R. (2001) *The Prime Minister in a Shrinking World*, Polity.

> ## Box 5.13 (continued)
>
> 'In the second term, the problem is the centralisation of power into the hands of the prime minister and an increasingly small number of advisors who make decisions in private without proper discussion. It is increasingly clear, I am afraid, that the cabinet has become, in Bagehot's phrase, a dignified part of the constitution…There is no real collective responsibility because there is no collective; just diktats in favour of increasingly badly thought through policy initiatives that come from on high.'
>
> Source: Clare Short's resignation speech, 12 May 2003.

Task 5.1

(a) Explain briefly how the notions of collective decision making in cabinet and collective cabinet responsibility are linked.

(b) Does it really matter that the doctrine of collective responsibility has been eroded?

Guidance

(a) Students often see these two terms as interchangeable. This is not the case, though any reading of the Ministerial Code (see Box 5.2) would suggest that the latter should be based firmly in the former. You should look to develop the argument that the increasing use of cabinet committees, 'bilaterals' and other extra-cabinet modes of decision making could be seen to have undermined the foundations of collective responsibility: if a minister is not at all involved in making a decision, it is harder to justify requiring him or her to stand by it. It might also be worth considering the question of 'leaks' and ministers secretly briefing the press in this context.

(b) Most commentators bemoan the decline of collective responsibility in the UK system. As we saw with the rise of the UK 'West Wing' in Task 3.2, however, such developments can also be seen as an inevitable function of broader changes in society. Put simply, it is no longer possible or desirable for all decisions to be taken in cabinet, and it is no longer reasonable, therefore, to expect ministers to resign over policies that they have never even had the opportunity to express a view on, let alone decide collectively.

Task 5.2

Study Box 5.3, which identifies the three roles traditionally attributed to cabinet. Using the rest of this chapter and any other material that you may have, write a brief paragraph on each role, outlining the relevant theory and examining the extent to which this role is still performed in practice.

Task 5.2 (continued)

Guidance

You might prefer to complete this task in the form of a table, with rows for each of the three roles and columns headed 'Theory' and 'Practice'. Whichever way you choose to present the material, it is important that you bring in relevant examples to illustrate developments in each of the three areas. You also need to be clear about who is performing such roles in areas where you conclude that the cabinet is no longer functioning.

Further reading

- Bennett, A. (2004) 'The UK and US cabinets', *Politics Review*, vol. 14, no. 2.
- Brady, C. and Catterall, P. (2000) 'Inside the engine room: assessing cabinet committees', *Talking Politics*, vol. 12, no. 3.
- James, S. (1996) 'The changing cabinet system', *Politics Review*, vol. 6, no. 2.
- Magee, E. and Garnett, M. (2002) 'Is cabinet government dead?', *Politics Review*, vol. 12, no. 1.
- Rathbone, M. (2003) 'The British cabinet', *Talking Politics*, vol. 16, no. 1.

Chapter 6

Do we have 'presidential government'?

The contemporary debate over prime minister–cabinet relations has its origins in Richard Crossman's introduction to the 1963 reprint of Walter Bagehot's *The English Constitution* (see Box 6.1) and was further fuelled with the posthumous publication of his *Diaries of a Cabinet Minister* in 1973. Prior to that point, remarkably little was known about the internal workings of the executive due to the fact that most of the key players had abided by the confidentiality element of the doctrine of collective responsibility.

Though the Radcliffe Report (1976) sought to put a lid on further revelations, Crossman's observations — specifically his contention that the UK was operating under a system of 'prime ministerial' as opposed to 'cabinet' government — became the subject of considerable debate in the 1980s and 1990s (see Box 6.2). The result has been the development of a number of alternative models that have sought to explain relations between the key players at the centre of government.

> Box 6.1
> ### The emergence of 'prime ministerial government'
> '…the post-war epoch has seen the final transformation of Cabinet Government into Prime Ministerial Government'.
>
> Source: from Richard Crossman's introduction to Walter Bagehot's *The English Constitution* (Fontana, 1963).

These models can be roughly divided into four broad categories:
1 prime ministerial models
2 presidential models
3 models that still stress the importance of the cabinet or, more often, the 'cabinet system'
4 core executive models

In this chapter we will examine each of these approaches to understanding prime minister–cabinet relations in order to address the question of whether or not the UK can truly be said to operate under a presidential system.

Box 6.2
The prime minister ascendant?

'John P. Mackintosh and Richard Crossman...asserted the existence of long-term trends that had progressively inflated the power of the Prime Minister and correspondingly diminished the position of the Cabinet as the supreme agent of government in the British Constitution. The Office [of prime minister] allowed its occupants to control government and party patronage; to have first access to the formidable network of government information, political intelligence and administrative direction embodied in the Cabinet Secretariat; to have the prior claim to speak for the government; and represent government to the public and through the mass media.'

Source: adapted from Foley, M. (1993) *The Rise of the British Presidency*, Manchester University Press.

Does the UK operate under prime ministerial government?

Crossman's contention that a growth in the powers and authority of the office of prime minister had led to the demise of cabinet government is firmly rooted in a number of significant truths (see Box 6.3). Others, such as Tony Benn in his 1980 work *Arguments for Socialism* and Lord Hailsham in his 1976 paper 'Elective dictatorship' and his Dimbleby Lecture of the same year (see Box 6.5), developed this theme further.

Box 6.3
What is prime ministerial government?

- The prime minister dominates the cabinet, as opposed to being simply *primus inter pares*.
- The prime minister claims a separate source of authority from his colleagues in government.
- The prime minister dominates the policy-making process.
- The prime minister acts as the principal spokesperson for the government.
- Departmental ministers must clear all key decisions with the prime minister before they are announced or brought to cabinet.
- The prime minister makes full use of the powers he has as quasi head of state.

Source: adapted from McNaughton, N. (2002) 'Prime ministerial government', *Talking Politics*, vol. 15, no. 1.

For Hailsham, in particular, the UK system had undergone a fundamental change in the 1960s and 1970s. Though he accepted that the uncodified, conventional basis of the UK executive always created a tendency towards **executive dominance** (see Box 6.4), these changes had led to a situation where this possibility had not only become a reality, but also become embodied in the singular figure of the prime minister — as opposed to the collective body of the cabinet. An extract from Hailsham's Dimbleby Lecture is given in Box 6.5.

Box 6.4

Executive dominance

- Governments commanding large Commons majorities are able to circumvent parliamentary procedure.
- The work of the majority party's whips and the imposition of guillotines on parliamentary debate allow governments to force through bills.
- The Lords' power to block government initiatives is limited by the Parliament Acts and by the Salisbury Doctrine. The Lords is, at best, a revising chamber.
- The powers of scrutiny held by UK standing committees and departmental select committees are weak in comparison to those exercised by US standing committees.

Source: Fairclough, P. in *UK Government and Politics Annual Survey 2006*, Philip Allan Updates.

Box 6.5

Hailsham on the dominance of the executive

'There has been a continuous enlargement of the scale and range of government itself [accompanied by] a change in the relative influence of the different elements in government, so as to place all the effective powers in the hands of one of them [i.e. the prime minister]. In other words, the checks and balances, which in practice used to prevent abuse, have now disappeared. [These] changes have operated in [one] direction — to increase the extent to which **elective dictatorship** is a fact, and not just a lawyer's theory.'

Source: Lord Hailsham (1976) 'The Richard Dimbleby Lecture', *The Listener*, 21 October.

Lord Hailsham

Does the UK operate under a presidential system?

Though talk of 'prime ministerial government' and 'elective dictatorship' still persists in the media (see Box 6.6), the debate has moved on somewhat in recent years with the suggestion that the prime minister has become a *de facto* president.

Box 6.6

An elective dictatorship?

'Cabinet government of the traditional model has manifestly atrophied over the past seven years, by deliberate neglect, not accident. Should we mind? If a collective cabinet system no longer functions well, and parliament is docile or impotent, we may be nearer to "elective dictatorship" than when Lord Hailsham coined the phrase a quarter of a century ago. Perhaps the country is content that the media should be the prime constraint upon highly centralised power. But the issues deserve public discussion.'

Source: Quinlan, M. (2004) 'Blair has taken us towards an elective dictatorship', the *Guardian*, 22 October.

The fact that both the 'prime ministerial' and 'presidential' models emphasise the importance of the increase in scope and extent of prime ministerial power has led some to see them as different stages on a single continuum – that is, a matter of degree rather than substance. In reality, however, the models differ in a number of important respects. Specifically, developments since Crossman and Hailsham made their comments, not least structural changes such as the emergence of a virtual Prime Minister's Department (see Chapter 3), and also the rise of the televisual media, have contributed greatly to the presidential thesis.

In his 1993 work, *The Rise of the British Presidency*, and in later books and articles, Michael Foley identified four characteristics which — in his view — justified the notion that the UK was moving towards a presidential system (see Box 6.7). Some of these themes were echoed in the work of writers such as Richard Rose, whose 2001 book, *The Prime Minister in a Shrinking World*, painted a picture of a premier who had been transformed by the role he was required to take on the world stage.

Box 6.7

Foley's thesis

Spatial leadership

The tendency for prime ministers to try and create visible distance between themselves and the machinery of government.

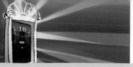

> **Box 6.7 (continued)**
>
> **Cult of the outsider**
>
> The tendency of prime ministers to characterise themselves as 'outsiders', fighting against formal structures and challenging 'business as usual'.
>
> **Public leadership**
>
> The way in which prime ministers have sought to appeal directly to the public through the modern mass media, thereby circumventing the normal channels.
>
> **The personal factor**
>
> The way in which prime ministers have become 'expanded personalities', personifying 'mass demands, common anxieties, social hopes and national ideals'.
>
> Source: Foley, M. (1994) 'Presidential politics in Britain', *Talking Politics*, vol. 6, no. 3.

Before we can examine the ideas of such writers more fully, we must examine what exactly we mean when we refer to the term 'presidential'.

What do we mean by the prime minister being 'presidential'?

As Foley observed: 'The "premiership", which has become an increasingly conventional term, is itself replete with suggestions of a singular office in form and substance.' This notion of a 'singular office' inevitably leads to comparisons being drawn between the UK prime minister and the US president. We should recognise, however, that the situation as regards the prime minister is a uniquely British one because of the way in which his or her powers originate, not in the limited ('checked') powers afforded the incumbent by a codified constitution, but in the assimilation of the unchecked prerogative powers formerly exercised by the monarch. Whereas talk of a 'presidential prime minister' appears, therefore, to suggest an increase in power, the US president's powers are in fact clearly circumscribed by the constitutional checks and balances instituted by the Founding Fathers, namely:

- Presidential appointments are subject to the 'advice' (following hearings) and 'consent' (confirmation by majority vote) of the US Senate.
- The president is not part of the legislature. Congress therefore has a far greater degree of independence over the passage of legislation and the approval of the budget. It can even pass laws without the president, where it can secure the two-thirds majority necessary to override the president's veto.
- There is no guarantee that the majority party in either the House or the Senate will be that of the president.

- The president must seek congressional approval for a declaration of war and a two-thirds majority in the Senate for the ratification of any treaties that the president may negotiate.
- The president has no formal role in the process by which the constitution is amended.
- Many aspects of policy are wholly beyond the reach of the president, often because they are determined at state level.

In all of these areas — whether through their position as head of the majority party in the Commons or through the exercise of prerogative powers — prime ministers have clearly always had a good deal more room for manoeuvre than their US counterparts. A number of authors have sought to address this paradox by suggesting that it might be more helpful to draw comparisons between the prime minister and the French president, for as Richard Rose noted, 'the Palais de l'Elysée is a constitutional "halfway" house between Number 10 and the White House, since France has a parliament and a prime minister as well as a president' (see Table 6.1).

French president Jacques Chirac

Table 6.1 'Presidencies' compared: UK, France and the USA

	Britain	France	USA
Media visibility	High	High	High
Route to top	Parliament	Civil service	Governor
Election	Party	Popular	Popular
Term	Insecure	Fixed: 5 years	Fixed: 4 years
Constitution	Unitary	Unitary	Federal
Checks	Slight, informal	Cohabitation	Congress, Supreme Court
Domestic policy	High	High	So-so
International policy	EU member	EU member	Super

Source: adapted from Rose, R. (2001) *The Prime Minister in a Shrinking World*, Polity.

Though such a debate is interesting, however, it is also something of a side issue, as the presidential thesis is rooted more in style and approach than it is in substance. Indeed, even those tangible changes that have occurred, in the Cabinet Office and the Prime Minister's Office for example, can be seen as a

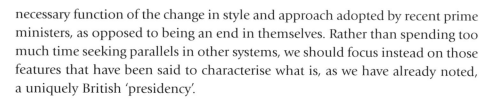
necessary function of the change in style and approach adopted by recent prime ministers, as opposed to being an end in themselves. Rather than spending too much time seeking parallels in other systems, we should focus instead on those features that have been said to characterise what is, as we have already noted, a uniquely British 'presidency'.

In what ways does Foley's thesis take the debate over prime ministerial power to a new level?

As we saw in Box 6.7, Foley's thesis can be divided into four broad and over-lapping themes.

Spatial leadership

Foley employed the term 'spatial leadership', a phrase more commonly applied to the study of US presidents, to describe the tendency for prime ministers to try and create what he called 'strategic space' between themselves and the other actors and institutions within the broader executive. The increased willingness of UK premiers to criticise government institutions publicly and, more importantly, their willingness to intervene in the broader public interest has, Foley maintained, separated and elevated the prime minister above other players at the heart of government. Foley cited the example of John Major, whose Citizen's Charter required public bodies to meet clearly defined targets in respect of service. Tony Blair's pursuit of his 'reform agenda' in the face of wide-ranging opposition within the executive branch and beyond might also be seen in this context. The ability of recent prime ministers to disassociate themselves from the government in this way allows them to exercise their prerogative powers to the full while at the same time avoiding full responsibility for anything that may go wrong. Inextricably linked to this notion of spatial leadership is the desire of recent prime ministers to portray themselves as political outsiders — the second key element of Foley's thesis.

Cult of the outsider

It has become increasingly common for politicians on both sides of the Atlantic to characterise themselves as political outsiders. In the USA, such a tendency was particularly in evidence in the 1990s with the presidential candidacies of both Ross Perot (a successful businessman) and Bill Clinton (the former Governor of Arkansas). Foley argued that individuals such as Carter (a one-time peanut farmer and former Governor of Georgia) and Reagan (a one-time Hollywood actor and former Governor of California) have also demonstrated a similar desire to portray themselves as Washington outsiders; anti-candidates.

Similarly, in the UK, leaders such as Thatcher and Major have been keen to play up their outsider credentials. Margaret Thatcher, a grammar school educated chemistry graduate and the daughter of a grocer, looked to distance herself from the old-school Tory patricians who constituted the larger part of her first cabinet. Major, who left school at 16 with only three O-levels and was the son of a former travelling showman, also emphasised his outsider credentials. Both premiers regarded themselves as anti-establishment figures with a mission to challenge deeply embedded assumptions and traditions. Though Blair's educational background and legal training made it harder for him to take on this kind of outsider role, we can see similar tendencies in his assault on Clause 4 of the Labour Party's constitution and his desire to challenge the power of the unions within the party.

Public leadership

The third element of Foley's thesis concerned the way in which US presidents and recent UK prime ministers have sought to go over the heads of other institutions in the government by appealing directly to the public, through their unique access to the media. In the USA, this willingness on the part of presidents to 'go public' — or 'wrap themselves in the flag' in times of war — has served to undermine the positions of those individuals who might otherwise limit the chief executive's power, while at the same time creating a direct bond between the leader and the broader citizenry. The emergence of a similar trend in the UK has gone some way towards addressing the problems caused by the fact that the prime minister, unlike the US president, is not directly elected. In addition, political parties themselves have an obvious interest in allowing their leaders to connect in this way (see Box 6.8).

Box 6.8

Prime ministers and public leadership

'The prime minister must have the ability to appeal to the public's own criteria for leadership…As parties are no longer reliable vehicles of public mobilisation in the more fluid conditions of dealigned and independent voters, they increasingly allow leaders off the collective leash. Each party does so in order to improve its chances of translating the leader's intermediary position with the public into the party's point of access into government.'

Source: Foley, M. (1994) 'Presidential politics in Britain', *Talking Politics*, vol. 6, no. 3.

Such tendencies are amply illustrated by the willingness of both the Labour Party (with Blair) and the Conservatives (with Cameron) to choose leaders whose particular skills were more suited to the task of engaging with the broader

public than they were to articulating the demands of their respective party's shrinking membership.

The personal factor

The cumulative effect of such tendencies has been the emergence of a prime minister who, as Foley put it in Box 6.7, has taken on an 'expanded personality' through his personification of 'mass demands, common anxieties, social hopes and national ideals'. Thus it was Margaret Thatcher, rather than the then defence secretary Francis Pym, who articulated the hopes and fears of a nation at the time of the Falklands War, and it was Blair, rather than the monarch, who captured the public mood in the wake of the death of Diana, Princess of Wales (see Chapter 1).

It is this role as 'public personality no. 1' (see Box 6.9) that both necessitated and at the same time justified the explosion in the number of personal staff working with and around the prime minister at No. 10 — particularly in the areas of communications and strategy. This, in turn, led some to go as far as to compare the prime minister in cabinet to the Hanoverian king at court (see Box 6.10).

Box 6.9

Public personality no. 1

'Today prime ministers and prime ministerial contenders speak more in the first person than they used to. Their health and mental fitness are openly discussed. Their parentage and origins, their childhood and formative experiences, their diets, tastes and pastimes, together with their wives and children, are all regarded as suitable subjects for exposure and assessment because they all help to convey that leadership is a personal resource.'

Source: Foley, M. (1994) 'Presidential politics in Britain', *Talking Politics*, vol. 6, no. 3.

Box 6.10

Cabinet or court?

'The pattern of recruitment and dismissal during the Blair years bears little resemblance to previous cabinet management in Britain. It is reminiscent of the factional fighting at the royal court in the eighteenth century. In the Hanoverian period, there was little or no ideological difference between the leading politicians. Their disagreements arose from personal ambition, and they fed off the habitual personal antagonism between the reigning monarch and his heir. Allegiances were based on a calculation of the life expectancy of the king.'

Source: Garnett, M. (2005) 'Still first among equals?', *Politics Review*, vol. 14, no. 4.

To what extent does Richard Rose accept Foley's presidential thesis?

Rose clearly agrees with many of the overriding themes of Foley's thesis, particularly in respect of the extent to which the media have afforded the modern premier a means by which to cultivate his or her popular appeal (see Box 6.11). Despite such areas of agreement, however, Rose does not accept the broader thesis in its entirety, arguing that 'To rely on television as a guide to government turns political leaders into celebrities. It confuses visibility on chat shows with authority conferred by constitutional office.'

Box 6.11

The new media-age prime minister

'To boost his "non-political" appeal to all the people, Tony Blair prefers soft television. Whereas Margaret Thatcher welcomed the opportunity of talking about policy even on chat shows, Blair is happy to chat about personal matters, which suits a philosophy of managed population…When Blair appeared on *This Morning with Richard and Judy*, described by television executives as 'Flopsy Bunny sofa TV', he mingled a discussion of the National Health Service and Northern Ireland with chat about his wife's swimsuit and the behaviour of his children.'

Source: Rose, R. (2001) *The Prime Minister in a Shrinking World*, Polity.

Rose accepts that the prime minister is now more 'first without equal' than *primus inter pares* on the domestic front. In what Rose dubs 'a shrinking world', however, the premier is 'no match for a president who plays hard ball' and will only ever be 'one among 15 [now 25] prime ministers' in the European Union. Thus, Rose concludes, 'the paradox of power is simply stated: at Westminster, the prime minister's power has increased significantly, but in the world beyond Dover it has greatly diminished'.

Has cabinet government been replaced by government under a cabinet system?

The sheer volume of material charting the rise of prime ministerial or presidential government in the UK might lead one to think that any notion of cabinet government has been laid to rest.

Authors such as George Jones of the London School of Economics, however, have rejected this basic premise. Though Jones has himself bemoaned the 'shirt-sleeve, sitting on the sofa, "call me Tony", chummy form of government', he argues that the notion of cabinet government is far from dead. He challenges Foley's assertion that parties have simply rolled over and deferred to the leader in the face of a dealigned electorate, arguing that the prospective prime minister's ability to connect personally with the broader public is only one element of the complex web of influences that determines the outcome of elections. Similarly, Jones's 'chairmanship model' (see Box 6.12) stresses the extent to which the broader party and the prospective, or serving, prime minister's frontbench colleagues still represent a considerable barrier to his or her individual ambitions; not least because they have the capacity to force policy changes (as with Thatcher over the exchange rate mechanism — see Chapter 2) or even force the premier out (e.g. Thatcher in 1990).

Box 6.12

The chairmanship model

'The most notable critic of Crossman's thesis [was] George Jones of the LSE. [Jones argued that though] the Prime Minister has a formidable range of powers...he is surrounded by major constraints. [He] is not a figure set apart but the leader of a group without whose support he is ineffective. The policy-making powers of the Prime Minister are limited partly because he can only be involved in a small proportion of government business and partly because his colleagues will protect their own departmental and political interests. Similarly, the party organisation does not simply do the Prime Minister's will.'

Source: adapted from Thomas, G. P. (1999) 'The prime minister and cabinet today', *Talking Politics*, vol. 11, no. 2.

Even those who accept that the traditional notion of cabinet government is dead, at least in respect of the idea of the cabinet as a single collective decision-making body, remain unconvinced by those who have attempted to elevate the prime minister above the other elements of the executive. For some, as we will see later in this chapter, it makes more sense to see the whole core executive as a complex web of interdependent actors and institutions, with policy resulting from an organic process of negotiation and compromise rather than at the command of a single omnipotent premier. For others, the cabinet remains crucial to the process, though the pressures of the modern age have necessitated its evolution from a single collective committee (Bagehot's 'hyphen that joined') to a more complex construction where the cabinet sits atop a system of ministerial committees and subcommittees. This cabinet system sees the cabinet take on a new, but equally important role to the one it once performed as the 'sounding board for a whole range of government policy' (see Box 6.13). In a sense we can see this stress on the cabinet system as something of a halfway house between the cabinet government model of yore and the core executive models advanced by writers such as R. A. W. Rhodes and Patrick Dunleavy, to which we turn our attention now.

Box 6.13

The 'cabinet system'

'From 1939 onwards the cabinet was compelled to delegate heavily to ministerial committees. Increasingly these committees have taken decisions on their own authority [see Chapter 5]. What this shows is that Britain is not governed by the cabinet but by a cabinet system, a highly articulated but diffuse organisation of which the cabinet is only the pinnacle. Though the cabinet itself now makes fewer decisions, however, ministers have been given greater opportunity to discuss broader policy issues during full cabinet meetings. The cabinet has, therefore, taken on a new guise as the sounding board for a whole range of government policy.'

Source: adapted from James, S. (1996) 'The changing cabinet system', *Politics Review*, vol. 6, no. 2.

The core executive model

In the same way that Foley sought to move away from the traditional debate over prime minister–cabinet relations by heralding the rise of a *de facto* presidential system in the UK, R. A. W. Rhodes and Patrick Dunleavy have examined the relative powers of the premier and cabinet in the broader context of relations within the core executive. As we saw in Chapter 4, this core executive is defined by Rhodes as 'a complex web of institutions, networks and practices surrounding the prime minister, cabinet, cabinet committees and their official counterparts, less formalised ministerial "clubs" or meetings, bilateral negotiations and interdepartmental committees. It also includes coordinating departments, chiefly the Cabinet Office, the Treasury, the Foreign Office, the law officers, and the security and intelligence services' (*Prime Minister, Cabinet and Core Executive*, 1995).

For writers such as Rhodes and Martin J. Smith (see Box 6.14), those who focus entirely on the fluid relationship between prime minister and cabinet fall into the trap of believing that power relationships within the core executive are based upon notions of 'command', whereas they are in fact rooted in mutual 'dependence'. As Smith recognises: 'In order to achieve goals, resources have to be exchanged. No single actor or institution can make policy separately' (see Table 6.2).

> ## Box 6.14
> ### Reframing the debate
>
> 'The argument over whether Britain has prime ministerial or cabinet government is misspecified for two simple reasons. First, its focus is too narrow and it ignores the range of institutions within the core executive which have a central role in policy-making. Second, it misunderstands the connections between the various actors and institutions within the core executive and so fails to recognise that the operation of the core executive is not about the prime minister commanding the actors but about building alliances, exchanging resources and adapting to prevailing circumstances.
>
> Power belongs neither to the cabinet nor to the prime minister; it is fluid, developing in the complex web of relationships within central government.'
>
> Source: adapted from Smith, M. J. (2000) 'The core executive', *Politics Review*, vol. 10, no. 1.

Table 6.2 Resources of the prime minister, ministers and officials

Prime minister	Ministers	Officials
Patronage	Political support	Permanence
Authority	Authority	Knowledge
Political support	Department	Time
Party political support	Knowledge	Whitehall network
Electorate	Policy networks	Control over information
Prime Minister's Office	Policy success	Keepers of the constitution
Bilateral policy making		

Source: adapted from Smith, M. J. (2000) 'The core executive', *Politics Review*, vol. 10, no. 1.

Moreover, the fact that much of what occurs within the core executive is based upon formal structures and practices — 'the rules of the game' — means that the part played by personality at the heart of government is less than one might think. The ability of key players to make best use of their resources and therefore the extent to which individual players are dependent upon one another will, of course, vary according to context and contingency. The underlying certainty, however, is that power is fragmented and progress is likely only when a sufficient number of players are brought on-board.

Though the prime minister's ability to 'go public' and 'hold court' may, therefore, create the illusion of a British presidency, the core executive model sees the premier as more of a 'line manager' (see Box 6.15), assigning roles and responsibilities, managing rivalries among middle managers, and trying to ensure that the bureaucratic 'tail' does not 'wag the dog'.

> Box 6.15
> **'President' or 'line manager'?**
>
> 'In one to one meetings Blair is in effect acting like a line manager, not a president. The very size, shape and architecture of No. 10 place natural limits on his powers. The increased growth in No.10 is…a symptom of weakness, rather than proof of strength — a number of prime ministers including Tony Blair have been unable to deliver as much as they would have liked.'
>
> Source: Jackson, N. (2003) 'The Blair style — presidential, bilateral or trilateral government?', *Talking Politics*, vol. 15, no. 2.

The greatest benefit of the core executive model is, of course, that it can accommodate those periods which appear to be indicative of 'prime ministerial' government (e.g. Thatcher, Blair) while at the same time allowing for the possibility that the cabinet may at times still appear to be the collective decision-making body it once was. This is because it sees the core executive as an organic structure in which the relationships between its constituent parts are fluid and ever evolving.

Conclusion

As we have seen throughout this book, it clearly makes more sense to frame discussions of prime ministerial power in terms of a growth in the office itself, relative to the other actors and institutions in the core executive, than it does to become overly focused on the relative success of individual incumbents. Thus, efforts to characterise the 'Major years' as evidence of a reassertion of cabinet government are no more valid than attempts to characterise the problems faced by US presidents such as Ford and Carter as evidence of a 'resurgent Congress' or an 'imperilled presidency'.

Put simply, the office of prime minister — like that of the US president — provides a potential for power; a potential that has been permanently enhanced by the interconnected developments outlined in Chapters 3 and 5. Whereas Asquith's contention that the office of prime minister is 'what the holder chooses and is able to make of it' still has some merit, the word 'able' should not be taken lightly. Whatever the individual 'abilities' of the incumbent — and few prime ministers remain totally on top of their game throughout their term in office — the premier does not operate in a vacuum. The extent to which prime ministers are 'able' to fulfil the potential of their office is, therefore, dependent not only on their own abilities, but also upon the political context and the presence or absence of capable ('able') rivals.

Chapter 6

Task 6.1

(a) Distinguish between notions of prime ministerial and presidential government in the UK context.

(b) Define the term 'elective dictatorship'. Illustrate your definition with suitable examples from your own studies.

Guidance

(a) Though these two terms are often taken as being different ways of expressing the same thing, there are clearly tangible differences, as well as obvious similarities, between the two theses. Your answer should identify the themes in the growth of the chief executive's power that both schools of thought hold in common, before moving on to consider the elements that make the presidential thesis distinct (e.g. notions of spatial leadership and the focus on media and style).

(b) You should define 'elective dictatorship' with reference to Hailsham's own words (see Box 6.5). It is important to recognise that Hailsham was not simply talking about the UK constitution's tendency towards executive dominance — through the governing party's control of the legislature — but also the upward concentration of such power in the hands of a single individual, the prime minister.

Task 6.2

A large part of the presidential thesis relates to the way in which the premier has become the focus for media attention. Take any quality newspaper over a working week (Monday to Friday).

(a) How many articles include the term 'prime minister' (PM) or the prime minister's name in the headline?

(b) How many articles relate to other named cabinet members?

(c) How many articles focus on the work of parliament?

(d) What does this tell us about the way in which the media cover events at Westminster?

Alternatively, complete the same task by watching the same television news programme over a 5-day period.

Guidance

It is important that you use the same newspaper (or television news broadcast) every day so that you can get a feel for the balance of coverage over a week. If you complete the newspaper survey *and* the television news survey, you could compare the weight of coverage given by different types of media. Similarly, a comparison of your results with those of a fellow student who has used a different newspaper or news channel might reveal evidence of bias in the media.

Task 6.3

Professor Neil Postman of New York University questioned whether or not the US president Abraham Lincoln would have been elected in a televisual age, in which 'what would be inside his head [i.e. his mind] wouldn't matter as much as what is outside [i.e. his physical appearance]'.

Which of the following characteristics are more important in a modern prime minister?

- intellectual ability
- relevant experience
- physical appearance
- charisma/personality and media savvy

Address each characteristic in your answer, illustrating the points you make with appropriate examples.

Guidance

In completing this task it might be helpful to think about the current leaders of the three main political parties as well as their closest rivals. In addition to your written comments, you might wish to give each individual a score out of 10 in each of the four areas identified. How would a leader such as Tony Blair compare to Gordon Brown? Was Menzies Campbell better qualified than those whom he beat in the race to replace Charles Kennedy as Liberal Democrat leader? How well did David Cameron score?

Further reading

- Ashbee, E. (2002) 'Parliamentary and presidential systems of government', *Politics Review*, vol. 11, no. 3.
- Foley, M. (1994) 'Presidential politics in Britain', *Talking Politics*, vol. 6, no. 3.
- Jackson, N. (2003) 'The Blair style — presidential, bilateral or trilateral government?', *Talking Politics*, vol. 15, no. 2.
- Jackson, N. (2004) 'Marketing man', *Politics Review*, vol. 13, no. 4.
- Riddell, P. (2006) 'Tony Blair: prime minister or president?', *Politics Review*, vol. 15, no. 3.
- Smith, M. J. (2000) 'The core executive', *Politics Review*, vol. 10, no. 1.

Glossary

agenda setting

The process by which various policies and ideas are prioritised. Governments seek to control the political agenda, though other political parties, the media and pressure groups are also said to play a part in this process.

Back to Basics campaign

Launched in 1993 by the then Conservative prime minister John Major, the Back to Basics campaign stressed the importance of individuals taking responsibility for their actions, though some mistook it as a defence of traditional moral and family values.

backbenchers

Those MPs representing major parties (in government or in opposition) who do not hold a senior responsibility for a particular area of policy. The term refers to the position of the benches upon which such individuals sit in the House of Commons. More senior colleagues sit on the front benches (e.g. as cabinet members, shadow cabinet members or frontbench spokespersons).

bilateral meetings (or 'bilaterals')

Where the prime minister chooses to discuss or even formulate policy through discussions with another individual minister, rather than through full discussions in cabinet.

Black Wednesday

Refers to 16 September 1992, when trading on the international money markets forced the UK out of the exchange rate mechanism. Many argue that the then chancellor Norman Lamont's failure to manage the crisis resulted in the Conservative Party losing its reputation for economic competence. See exchange rate mechanism.

Butler Report (2004)

Completed by the former cabinet secretary, Lord Butler, the report reviewed the process by which intelligence regarding weapons of mass destruction was handled and communicated in advance of the joint UK/US invasion of Iraq in 2003. Lord Butler also made a number of more general observations regarding the way in which government appeared to operate under Tony Blair.

cabinet committees

Smaller groupings of cabinet ministers chosen by the prime minister to consider particular areas of policy or individual policies before reporting back to cabinet proper. Permanent ('standing') or temporary ('ad hoc'), the importance of such bodies lies in the fact that their decisions are rarely overturned by the full cabinet.

cabinet government

The traditional view that decision-making power within government rests with the cabinet, while the prime minister merely acts as chair — *primus inter pares* (first among equals). In recent decades, this notion has been questioned by those who feel that the UK operates under a 'prime ministerial' or 'presidential' system of government.

Cabinet Office

Originally a body consisting of a number of secretariats which coordinated the work of those civil servants employed in supporting the work of cabinet. In recent years the Cabinet Office and the Prime Minister's Office have expanded and become interwoven to the point where some have heralded the rise of a virtual 'Prime Minister's Department'.

cabinet secretary

The senior civil servant who formally heads the Cabinet Office.

cabinet system

Refers not only to the cabinet itself but also to the various committees and other bodies that operate around it. A more complex model of the modern cabinet, it lends credence to the view that cabinet government is not dead, but has instead evolved to meet the demands of a new age.

checks and balances

Often used with reference to the US system of government, the idea that those in the executive, legislature and judiciary have the means to frustrate one another's ambitions. Powers are shared in such a way that the various branches of government must cooperate for anything of substance to be achieved. In the UK, the absence of a codified and entrenched constitution is said to limit the effectiveness of such checks, thereby favouring executive dominance.

chief of staff

Since 1997, a political appointee who has the lead role in coordinating the efforts of those who work in the Prime Minister's Office.

Citizen's Charter

John Major's flagship policy of 1991, which sought to ensure clear targets for the quality of public service provision. Replaced by Labour's 'Service First' initiative in 1998.

codified constitution

A single, authoritative, entrenched document that sets out the composition and powers of the various institutions of state, the relationships between these institutions, and the relationship between the state and its citizens.

collective responsibility

The convention by which all cabinet members are required to publicly stand by those decisions made privately within cabinet meetings — regardless of whether or not they themselves agreed with the decision taken — or resign. In recent years this convention has been extended to cover ministers below cabinet rank.

convention

A practice that is generally accepted and observed without having legal status.

core executive

The network of institutions, advisory bodies and key individuals at the heart of government that contribute to the policy-making process.

de facto

Literally, 'in fact'; regardless of the presence or absence of legal authority. Contrast with *de jure*, meaning according to rightful (legal) entitlement.

Director of Communications

A position first held by Alastair Campbell in the UK. The individual charged with the responsibility of managing the government's relations with the media. Evolved from the role of press secretary following the 2001 general election.

elective dictatorship

A phrase coined by Lord Hailsham in 1976. Refers to the way in which the power and authority of parliament is concentrated in the hands of any party leader who possesses and can control a sizeable majority in the House of Commons. Synonymous with notions of executive dominance.

exchange rate mechanism

An attempt to control fluctuations in the relative value of European currencies ahead of the introduction of the euro. See Black Wednesday.

executive dominance

In the absence of a formal separation of powers and a system of entrenched checks and balances, the notion that the UK executive is able to use its Commons majority to control the legislature. See elective dictatorship.

Falklands War (1982)

A short war in which the UK defeated an Argentinian force that had invaded the Falkland Islands in support of longstanding territorial claims.

impeachment

A process by which an elected politician, judge or other official can be removed for treason or other high crimes.

incumbent

The individual currently in office.

individual ministerial responsibility

The convention that cabinet ministers are answerable for their personal conduct (personal responsibility) and at the same time responsible for all that is done within their departments (role responsibility). Under this convention, ministers failing in either sphere are expected to offer their resignation.

kitchen cabinet

A smaller, looser grouping of cabinet colleagues, advisors and friends that a prime minister may prefer to discuss policy decisions with, outside of formal cabinet structures.

Liaison Committee

Comprising the chair of each Commons select committee, the Liaison Committee plays a role in coordinating the activities of individual committees. It benefited from an enhanced public profile after 2001 when Prime Minister Tony Blair agreed to be questioned by the committee every 6 months.

loans for peerages affair

The scandal that surrounded the suggestion that senior figures in the Labour Party had offered the promise of peerages and other honours to those who agreed to make loans to the party ahead of the 2005 general election. Such loans circumvented the rules that had previously been introduced in respect of donations.

Maastricht Treaty (1992)

The treaty that saw the European Economic Community transformed into the European Union. Maastricht set out a timetable for the creation of a single

European currency but also extended the Community into areas such as justice and home affairs, foreign and security policy.

Ministerial Code

Known as 'Questions of Procedures for Ministers' prior to 1997. This document sets out the roles and responsibilities of a government minister. The Code includes a number of paragraphs that seek to formalise notions of collective decision making and collective responsibility.

Night of the Long Knives

Refers to the day on which the Conservative prime minister Harold Macmillan removed around one-third of his cabinet in July 1962.

1922 Committee

A body comprising all Conservative backbench MPs that seeks to keep senior MPs in the party in touch with opinion in the broader party.

No. 10

Literally, the official residence of the prime minister in Downing Street, London. Also a term used to refer to the Prime Minister's Office.

Parliamentary Labour Party

A body comprising all Labour Party MPs.

patronage

In the context of this book, the prime minister's power to 'hire and fire'.

poll tax

Formally known as the 'community charge', a tax levied on every adult as a means of part-funding local government services. Introduced in Scotland in 1989 and in the rest of the UK in 1990. Anti-poll tax protests contributed to Margaret Thatcher's fall from power in 1990. The tax was replaced by the council tax, a property-based tax, in 1993.

Prime Minister's Department

A body that some commentators argue should be created in order to provide the modern prime minister with the support necessary to discharge his or her duties effectively. Some argue that changes in the nature and organisation of bodies such as the Cabinet Office and the Prime Minister's Office have already seen the creation of what amounts to a Prime Minister's Department.

Prime Minister's Office

Not a room in the sense of the US 'Oval Office' but instead a collection of bodies and individuals supporting the work of the prime minister. Populated by a blend of appointees, career civil servants and special advisors, the PMO now numbers over 150 staff.

Prime Minister's Questions

Introduced by Harold Macmillan in 1961, this was originally a twice-weekly 15-minute slot where MPs could table questions for the prime minister. Since 1997, a single 30-minute slot on Wednesday has replaced the shorter sessions on Tuesday and Thursday. This was heralded as a change that would provide more considered scrutiny of the prime minister and limit the tendency towards 'yah-boo' politics.

prime ministerial government

Bringing into question notions of cabinet government, a theory that sees the prime minister as having assumed a dominant position within the executive.

primus inter pares

Literally, 'first among equals'. The notion that the prime minister merely acts as a chairperson within cabinet. See cabinet government.

quangos

An acronym referring to quasi-autonomous non-governmental organisations: quasi (or semi) autonomous (independent) because such bodies tend to work with a degree of independence when delivering a specific area of public service; non-governmental because their members are not normally drawn from the ranks of elected politicians or the civil service, despite the fact that they are state funded. Some prefer to use terms such as NDPBs (non-departmental public bodies) and EGOs (extra-governmental organisations).

royal prerogative

The constitutional powers formally held by the monarch but in practice exercised by the prime minister.

scrutiny

The process of critical examination by which government institutions are held accountable. It is said to be a key function of parliament and also of the mass media.

separation of powers

A process by which the three branches of government — executive, legislature and judiciary — are formally separated. Though such a separation of powers is entrenched in the US system, the UK is normally said to operate under a system of fused powers, with the executive sitting in the legislature.

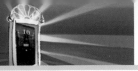
sofa-government

A phrase used to describe the way in which Tony Blair was said to have directed government through a series of informal and unminuted bilateral meetings conducted on the sofas at No. 10.

special advisors

Special advisors proliferated after 1997 as a means of making the government less reliant on the work of the regular civil service. They also help the prime minister to keep abreast of developments in government departments that are often far better staffed and resourced. Although such advisors are nearly always paid as civil servants, they are political appointees rather than career civil servants. Special advisors do not, therefore, have to conform to the traditional civil service principles of impartiality, anonymity and permanence.

stalking horse

A candidate who, though unlikely to succeed, challenges an incumbent (e.g. a party leader) as a means of paving the way for a more realistic contender. For example, Anthony Meyer's challenge to Conservative leader Margaret Thatcher in 1989 prepared the ground for Michael Heseltine's challenge the following year.

statute

A law passed by the UK parliament. The supreme source of the UK constitution.

subpoena

A writ requiring an individual to attend a court.

vote of confidence

A vote of those MPs present, held at the end of a debate on a motion declaring that the House of Commons has no confidence in the government of the day. Convention dictates that a government losing such a vote is required to resign, prompting a general election.

Westland affair (1985)

A scandal surrounding arguments over the procurement of military helicopters by the UK government. The then defence secretary, Michael Heseltine, walked out of a cabinet meeting, later resigning, when he was prevented from appealing against an earlier decision taken in committee. Leon Brittan, the then secretary of state for trade and industry, was subsequently forced to resign after he admitted instructing a civil servant to leak a memo that had undermined Heseltine's position.

whip

A party officer appointed to maintain discipline within the parliamentary party under the guidance of a chief whip. The term 'whip' also refers to the written document produced by each party's whips that instructs MPs to attend parliament and vote in a particular way. The importance that the party attaches to particular parliamentary votes is indicated by the number of times they are underlined on this documentary whip — hence the term 'three-line whip'.

Whipless Wonders

A collective term applied to the eight Conservative backbench MPs who had the party whip withdrawn in 1994 as a result of their voting against the European Communities (Finance) Bill.